# Sustainable School Improvement

# Sustainable School Improvement

## Fueling the Journey with Collective Efficacy and Systems Thinking

Patricia Wright

ROWMAN & LITTLEFIELD

*Lanham • Boulder • New York • London*

Published by Rowman & Littlefield
An imprint of The Rowman & Littlefield Publishing Group, Inc.
4501 Forbes Boulevard, Suite 200, Lanham, Maryland 20706
www.rowman.com

86-90 Paul Street, London EC2A 4NE



British Library Cataloguing in Publication Information Available

**Library of Congress Cataloging-in-Publication Data Available**

ISBN 978-1-4758-6286-7 (cloth)
ISBN 978-1-4758-6287-4 (paperback)
ISBN 978-1-4758-6288-1 (electronic)

∞™ The paper used in this publication meets the minimum requirements of American National Standard for Information Sciences—Permanence of Paper for Printed Library Materials, ANSI/NISO Z39.48-1992.

*To my grandchildren who fuel my passion for fostering educational systems that embrace meaningful collaboration as a way to ensure that every child has a successful learning journey.*

# Contents


Foreword ix

Preface xiii

Acknowledgments xv

**1** The CAR Framework: Fueling Connections 1

**2** Is Your GPS Working? Curriculum as the Master Learning Plan 11

**3** Supporting a Culture of Collaboration 29

**4** Ensuring a Smooth Journey: Collaboratively Improving School Climate 39

**5** Leading the CAR Journey toward the Ultimate Destination 53

Appendix A: Summary of Roadblock and Forward Thinking 67

Appendix B: 10 PLC Conversations 69

Appendix C: Unpacking a Standard Worksheet 73

Appendix D: CAR Instructional Unit Template 75

Appendix E: Guide to Developing the CAR Instructional Unit Plan 77

Appendix F: The Important Role of Classroom Assessments and Common Assessments 81

Appendix G: Professional Expectations of Educators at School 83

Appendix H: Group Norms Reflection 85

Appendix I: Individual Norms Reflection 87

Appendix J: Mission Statement 89

Appendix K: The Professional Climate: What Is Our Current Reality? 91

Appendix L: 10 School Climate Team Conversations 95

Appendix M: The 14 Dimensions of School Climate Measured by the CSCI 97

Appendix N: The CAR Planning Guide 99

Appendix O: The CAR Rubric 101

Appendix P: Crosswalk: Standards for Professional Learning Summary and the CAR 115

Appendix Q: Leadership Roles within CAR 121

Appendix R: Statement of Vision and Commitment 125

About the Contributors 127

About the Author 129

# Foreword

Michael Fullan gave us *The Right Drivers*. Roland Barth likened leadership to sailing. Dennis Shirley and I set out *The Fourth Way* of educational change. Great leaders, and leaders of leaders, understand that a significant element of effective leadership involves describing an important and even epic journey we must all undertake to escape from darkness, bondage, or any other existential threat to reach a better place together. Whether it's *The Greek Odyssey, The Lord of the Rings, The Pilgrim's Progress,* or the animated children's movie, *Moana,* narratives of epic journeys describe how a group can seek and reach a better life together despite obstacles that might get in the way and distractions that can easily take them off course.

In this book, Patricia Wright and her colleagues use another quest-like metaphor, *The Connected Action Roadmap,* or CAR, to show how schools can bring about school improvement and transformation that can benefit all students everywhere. Once you are in the CAR, they show, you will need a driver, a GPS and all the other tools that will help you find your way and reach your destination. As you read this big educational road trip of a book, you'll also learn it has a great soundtrack—key ideas, and inspiring quotes from some of the leading thinkers in teaching, learning, assessment, leadership, and change.

The CAR is a big-picture roadmap, but it also has a very detailed cartographic legend. This is set out in clear guides for constructive conversations about specific practices, such as unpacking standards, or identifying norms for effective collaboration. CAR alerts you not to get distracted by dysfunctional routines such as allowing bad behavior to pass without comment and not to become prey to the siren-like seductions of deceptively alluring workshop presentations.

Who wants a big-picture book now, even if it does have lots of tools and guidelines too? We're just coming out of a pandemic, hopefully. Teachers and leaders are struggling just to get normal classroom life going without masks and interruptions. Why don't we just all get on with the jobs that were stolen from us and leave all this blue-sky thinking until later?

Let me explain why by pointing out the impact and implications of just four things that are occupying my mind and my time on Valentine's Day, 2022.

First, my city of Ottawa, the capital of Canada, is under occupation by thousands of demonstrators in trucks and other vehicles, ostensibly protesting vaccine mandates, even though the plan was first constructed on Facebook in 2019! Nazi and confederate flags have been flown, local residents have been abused, the national war memorial has been desecrated, and saunas and dance stages have been set up outside parliament. There has been no significant police intervention, in the hope that it might all dissipate spontaneously. It didn't, though, because in this nation's capital, just like any junior high school, bad behavior doesn't terminate itself. And so now, for the first time in Canadian history, the Emergency Powers Act has been invoked. Democracy, civility, decency, and community are all in peril, even in Canada—reminding us that democracy does not take care of itself. The world is falling off its axis, and how we educate our young, and with what purpose, beyond basics and test scores, is a huge part of that. The big picture of where we are all headed is no longer just the concern of intellectuals and media pundits; it's everyone's problem now.

Second, I am preparing to address a national task force that has been convened by the American Federation of Teachers, to address the future of teaching at a time of massive problems of recruitment and retention in the profession. Teachers are worn out. Many are leaving and taking their skills to higher paid jobs in the economy elsewhere. Teachers are part of COVID-19's Great Resignation. What might turn things around? Higher pay will help, as will proper professional certification. But a few mindfulness seminars, yoga sessions, or days devoted to social and emotional learning for teachers almost certainly won't. Teachers will stay in teaching when the work feels better, when they are not micromanaged, when they have more autonomy over their own judgments, when they have more time for the authentic collegiality described in this book, and when they don't have to teach things that they don't believe in for high stakes tests that have little educational value. The culture of collegiality, of PLCs that fosters inspiring and instructive conversations that improve practice, are a vital part of the CAR.

Third, COVID-19 has had some terrible consequences for our schools and our kids in terms of lost learning and damaged well-being. Yet it has also shone a light on the possibility that things can be better once COVID-19 is truly over. I'm in the middle of reviewing the Irish education system and its handling of assessment changes during the pandemic, and it's clear that we have all learned a lot. We've learned that change can be quick. It doesn't always have to be slow. Teachers have picked up new digital skills, including ones that involve new ways of providing assessment and feedback. State after state in the United States is now considering whether it is finally time to abandon high stakes standardized achievement tests in favor of better forms of assessment of the kind described by this book's authors. Teachers have collaborated more than they used to, because the moral imperative of pandemic circumstances, not the mandates of governments and administrators, have forced them to—and more widespread, authentic forms of collaborative professionalism are now within our grasp. Parents have also watched educators teach online, almost every day in some cases, and they are not going to want to be returned to two meetings a year in a gymnasium with their teenagers' teachers. Everything we thought couldn't be changed is suddenly up for grabs. The big picture belongs to all of us. It's time to dream big and act boldly together.

Last, in the depths of the pandemic, seven colleagues and I at the University of Ottawa, felt that people needed an uplifting narrative and journey of learning, well-being and change as we emerged from the pandemic. So, with the help of $2.7m from the LEGO Foundation, we are constructing a national network of 40 schools using play-based learning, outdoors, on screen, and/or in makerspaces (green, screen, and machine), beyond Grade 3, with high needs populations, to get students re-engaged, and, in some cases, engaged for the first time, with their learning, in powerful ways. In each participating province (the Canadian equivalent of a state), six diverse schools will be connected to a senior system leader, embedding the networks within policy. It's a strategy to develop creativity, but it's also a creative way to rethink policy. It's all about coherence, as this book's authors would say, without top-down alignment.

Coming out of a crisis is a time to do more than breathe a sigh of relief. It's a time to rethink our work and our lives, to take responsibility for the big picture rather than just tweaking things we think are otherwise out of our control. It's about working with each other for a common good rather than having politicians and administrators constantly telling us what to do. And it's about acting quickly, changing fast, and getting from talk into action with a collective sense of urgency.

We're in the *Amazing Race* for better schools in a better world. It's a race with roadblocks and detours, for sure. But it's also a race that will only have value if there are no eliminations, and if everyone stays in and with their CAR until the very end.

This book is not pie in the sky. It's about making every educator a systems thinker and a systems doer. As the interim superintendent of a public school district is quoted as saying: "Rather than looking at work on many different priorities as new initiatives, the CAR framework connects them altogether into one cohesive framework to drive school improvement efforts." If we don't pull together, now more than ever, things will simply fall apart. Reintroduced mandates will suck the life out of teaching. Conversations will drift into thin air. Teachers' disrupted lives have shown them that other rewarding work options are out there. We need to work to re-engage our students, and we need to re-engage our teachers too. Working in a system that is mission-driven, coherent, and collaboratively developed will create a job that makes sense, provides pleasure, and has a rewarding impact. The CAR framework will help everyone reading this book to get to that very special place.

Andy Hargreaves
University of Ottawa
February 2022

# Preface

School improvement—how many times have we heard this phrase? In my experiences as a teacher and school and district leader, it seemed as though achieving a cycle of continuous school improvement was akin to finding the Holy Grail. As a teacher for 21 years, I had experienced a whirlwind of initiatives and programs all aimed at improving student achievement. The programs and initiatives were rarely sustained and I, like many of my colleagues, felt at the mercy of the newest "next best thing." As this pattern continued, we felt we were no longer in control of our practice. It now belonged to the next vendor or next consultant with the "guaranteed answer." Conversations were more about programs and compliance, not practice and process. Feelings of self-efficacy dwindled and self-survival kicked in. I found myself in a constant state of wondering if there was a better way, a better route to improving outcomes for all students.

As I prepared to take on my first formal leadership role, I turned to the wealth of available professional resources and reviewed the educational research of such amazing thought leaders as Andy Hargreaves, Michael Fullan, Grant Wiggins and Roland Barth to name just a few. My lens was always this, "How can I operationalize this information into a system that supports a direct route to the Holy Grail?" How could I break away from a dependence on outside forces and return ownership for learning to the educators? How could our school collectively focus on student learning and together, as Roland Barth encouraged, improve our school from within?

The Connected Action Roadmap (CAR) evolved as a result of these wonderings. The CAR is not another program. It is a process that helps schools focus on what matters most. It relies on building the collective efficacy of educators through meaningful and impactful collaboration. The CAR requires educators to adopt new ways of working together. This means challenging roadblock thinking, some very long-held assumptions about the ways we have always done things. The CAR is not a quick fix or a Band-Aid approach to school improvement. Instead, it represents a journey, one that can continuously strengthen teaching, leading and learning. The CAR can help get your school to slow down, step off the merry-go-round of initiatives, and build the professional capital that supports student success.

The CAR has received the support of all the major educational associations in New Jersey. The Foundation for Educational Administration, the professional development arm of the New Jersey Principals and Supervisors Association, is working with dozens of districts and hundreds of schools throughout the state who have chosen to implement this framework.

As the author of the framework, the CAR proved a successful strategy for me as a school leader, however, I did not know how other schools would react to the messages in this book. The CAR is based on the work of esteemed educational authors and researchers known to many educators. Despite my own experiences in several districts, I wondered if other educators might view the messages of CAR as something they "already knew." Well, they may have known about Wiggins' Backward Design, Fullan's Coherence Framework and Rick Dufour's emphasis on PLCs. Many had read Andy Hargreaves' work related to professional capital or John Hattie's research on collective efficacy. However, we have not worked with one school yet, who is not intrigued by how the CAR operationalizes these concepts in a systemic process of school improvement. "This makes so much sense," is often their first reaction. Educators connected with the purpose of the framework and could list the benefits of its implementation. Yet, we have witnessed through our intensive work with schools, the struggle leaders have in shifting away from, "the way we have always done things," even if they may realize that way is not built on sound educational practice. Their worlds have become layer upon layer of initiatives and programs. Teachers are overwhelmed and often comment on the lack of time to do their "real work."

These schools have to face the challenge of refocusing. They must rebuild the structures that are part of the CAR Framework. They must make the time for authentic professional collaboration. They must reorder priorities and commit to a long-term plan of action to strengthen the components of the CAR framework. They must get back to basics and stop letting change, for change's sake, be the distraction that derails their efforts. They must recognize that doing all these things is actually messy and harder than just reaching outside of their school building for an easier answer. The rewards, however, are great. Once the foundation is built, educators and school leaders will begin to see themselves as the experts. They will be more selective and purposeful about the programs and initiatives they adopt. They will look at compliance mandates through a new lens. What is the purpose of the mandate? How can it help us to strengthen our work? How can we comply in a way that does not take our focus off the destination and disrupt our journey?

The pandemic certainly has presented unprecedented challenges. In our work with schools, we learned that those that had the structures provided in the CAR framework faced them together and sustained their focus on student learning and student well-being.

Throughout the book, you will have an opportunity to hear from educators and school leaders in schools that are implementing the processes within the CAR framework. You can begin to challenge your own roadblock thinking and use the tools provided to determine how you might best begin a coherent school improvement journey.

# Acknowledgments

I want to express my sincere gratitude to my co-authors and friends, Emil Carafa, Brian Chinni, Vicki Duff, and Donna McInerney. The CAR emphasizes the importance of collegiality and collaboration and you model that in everything you do. Thank you for your ongoing wisdom and support. A special thanks to Stacy Barksdale-Jones, professional assistant extraordinaire. Your patience and kindness during the preparation of the manuscript was invaluable.

I also want to thank all of the professional associations in New Jersey who have supported the CAR for many years. My deepest appreciation to the Overdeck Family Foundation, the Sands Foundation and the New Jersey Department of Education for their commitment to funding the CAR pilots schools.

Finally, I want to thank all the educators and school and district leaders who have implemented the CAR framework. Your strong commitment to this work has enabled us to have a deep understanding of the challenges you face every day, as well as the courage and commitment required to embrace forward thinking.

## *Chapter 1*

# The CAR Framework

## *Fueling Connections*

> CAR was the answer to several school and district needs to improve teaching and learning through: job-embedded professional learning for staff in unpacking and understanding standards; standards-based and aligned instruction; equity for learners across classrooms; a culture for collaborative instructional improvement and more effective use of Professional Learning Communities (PLC) time. Underlying all of this is the current pressing need to address the opportunity gap and improve outcomes for under-served populations.
>
> —Jeannine Lanphear, Supervisor of Math & Science,
> North Brunswick Public Schools

Despite the plethora of educational research and the adoption of new programs, innovative technology and abundant resources, schools often fail to create a continuous cycle of school improvement. Instead, the cost of failed initiatives and the damage resulting from decades of well-meaning "recycled efforts" and ill-advised political solutions has created a sense of urgency to embrace a systemic way of thinking, one that returns ownership for the practice of education to the professionals in every school.

The Connected Action Roadmap (CAR) is not a program; it is not an initiative. In fact, CAR was developed to address the much deeper problem caused by the volume of programs and initiatives implemented in schools. It is not uncommon to hear a teacher say, "I can't focus on the kids; there are just too many things to do. I'm overwhelmed." Has change itself become a distraction? Has it forced educators to move not toward but away from their primary focus—student learning?

As schools have sought answers from vendors and outside "experts," educators have lost more and more ownership of their practice. Because they are inundated with the "latest new best thing" or engaged in meeting compliance mandates driven by external forces including federal and state mandates, they have been conditioned to act in ways that are often contrary to sound educational practice. Educators' actions are driven by faulty assumptions that keep schools stuck in a vicious cycle, not a cycle of continuous improvement. These assumptions referred to as "roadblock thinking" reinforce a system driven by compliance and drowning in a sea of initiatives with little return on investments in programs. Assumptions are not necessarily what educators deeply believe but they reflect the ways the system "has always done things." Unless challenged and replaced with an agreed-upon set of beliefs, the assumptions continue to be barriers to effective change. Throughout the book, the reader will have the opportunity to challenge roadblock thinking, and shift gears to embrace "forward thinking" that will support the implementation of effective educator practice and a coherent process for school improvement (see Appendix A).

CAR helps school leaders operationalize coherence-making by refocusing efforts on the key elements of effective schools. It is the connections between those elements—school culture, curriculum, instruction, assessment, professional learning and teacher and principal effectiveness that are key. Understanding how they are connected is essential, otherwise, we once again see the actions we take to strengthen each component as disparate. In other words, just one more thing.

CAR is not based on revolutionary ideas. It was developed by a practitioner who was witnessing the devastating effects of initiative fatigue on the school community. The power of the model comes from providing a way to operationalize the existing research and utilize current knowledge about school improvement within a school or district-wide process that actually results in the desired change.

## UNDERSTANDING THE COMPONENTS OF CAR

Figure 1.1 shows a graphic representation of the CAR model. Let's begin with a broad examination of each component of CAR, why it is important and how it is connected to the other components. It is important to again emphasize that CAR is not a program but a process. It is best explained through the metaphor of a journey. As you know,

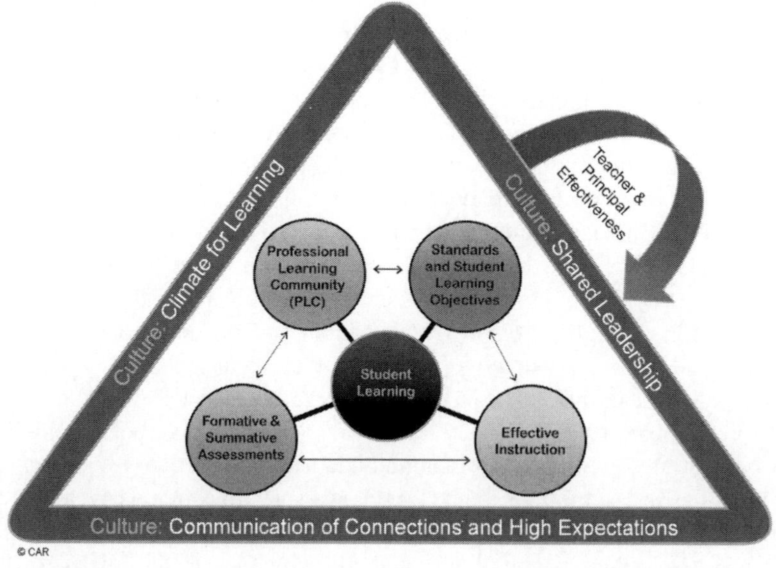


**Figure 1.1 CAR Model.**

there are many routes to a destination. CAR was built to acknowledge that the decisions about which routes to follow belong to the educators taking the journey. This reflects a shift in thinking from the idea that programs and initiatives brought into the school will improve outcomes, and instead acknowledges that those implementing the process are the only ones who can improve outcomes. As Roland Barth noted, "Too much emphasis has been placed on reforming school from the outside through policies and mandates. Too little has been paid to how schools can be shaped from within" (Barth, 1991).

## The Destination

Although schools are starting their own unique journeys from various locations, every school is focused on the same destination—student learning. How do the educators and administrators in a school keep the focus on student learning? In order to answer this question, examine the first example of roadblock thinking.

**Roadblock Thinking: Principals can and should be direct instructional leaders.**

Educators hear a lot about how principals need to move away from the role of manager and transition to the role of instructional leader. What is instructional leadership and exactly how can principals make this shift? Consider this quote from Michael Fullan:

> Principals' responsibilities have increased enormously over the past two decades. They are expected to run a smooth school; manage health, safety, and the building; innovate without upsetting anyone; connect with students and teachers; be responsive to parents and the community; answer to their districts; and above all, deliver results. More and more, they are being led to be direct instructional leaders.

How does a principal do it all? Consider the next part of that quote,

> and therein lies the rub. How is this for a shocker: the principal as direct instructional leader is not the solution! If principals are to maximize their impact on learning, we must reconceptualize their role so that it clearly, practically, and convincingly becomes a force for improving the whole school and the results it brings. (Fullan, 2014)

Stop assuming that the principal can effectively do it all and consider the principal as the architect of structures that allow for shared instructional leadership.

**Forward Thinking: Principals must empower those who directly impact student learning every day—the teachers. They are the direct instructional leaders.**

Principal instructional leadership is best defined as the ability to establish, monitor and sustain a collaborative system that allows teachers and principals to share leadership and accountability for improving student learning. The CAR process provides the path to building true instructional leadership at every level.

## The Vehicle

CAR promotes shared leadership for learning through the engagement of teachers and school leaders in the collaborative examination of instructional practice in authentic PLCs. PLCs are the vehicle that will move educators closer to the collective destination, but only if their purpose is clear and their work leads to higher levels of student learning. It has been the experience of the authors that, like many well-intended mandates, PLCs have been misinterpreted. The term PLC is often viewed as a dirty word because PLCs can exist in name only and when misused are, frankly, considered a waste of teachers' valuable time.

As Rick Dufour has long professed, PLCs provide the opportunity for educators to engage in collaborative inquiry, problem-solving, and reflection on their practice for the ultimate benefit of student learning (Dufour, 2004*)*.

What should teams be inquiring about? What problems are they uncovering and what processes will help them reach the best solution? What exactly is the practice upon which they should be reflecting? How does their work impact student learning?

Now consider this quote:

> Well-intentioned people will be unable to implement the PLC process unless they have a deep, shared understanding of the conditions they are attempting to create, the ideas that should drive their work and the obstacles they are likely to encounter as they move forward. (DuFour and Fullan, 2013)

Because some leaders have faulty ideas related to the purpose and function of PLCs, implementation in many schools is uneven at best. Many educators find themselves forced to meet in groups that are having little impact on their practice or their students' learning. This confusion around purpose has often resulted in a negative connotation of collaborative teaming. Within the CAR framework, the PLC follows a conversational process that ensures it functions effectively as the vehicle that moves all students closer to the destination—improved learning outcomes.

One of the underlying principles of CAR is that the practice of education is based on a strong knowledge of curriculum, instruction and assessment. CAR utilizes ten specific conversations that drive inquiry, problem-solving and reflection on the curriculum that educators are delivering, the instruction they are providing and the assessment data they are collecting. Engaging consistently in these conversations results in meaningful changes in practice. Effective PLC conversations impact student achievement by impacting teacher practice. They allow educators to develop, implement, and reflect on a viable and equitable curriculum. The conversations, discussed in detail in chapter 2, give the PLC a clear purpose and direction for their work. Educators' collective growth becomes continuous as focused collaboration strengthens their ability to continually and tactically respond to the needs of all the students they serve.

PLCs need more than clarity about their role. They need to exist in a collegial climate that will effectively allow them to not only engage deeply in the 10 conversations, but make the instructional decisions that result from their work. For this reason, chapter 3 will focus on the components of a collegial climate for adult professional learning.

By supporting a collaborative culture, by providing consistent time for educators to engage in these targeted conversations, by fully participating in the dialogue, and ensuring the conversations lead to changes in practice, the principal demonstrates strong instructional leadership becoming "a force for improving the whole school and the results it brings."

## The Map or GPS: Capturing the Conversations

If the PLC conversations are to move teachers in the right direction, they will need a map that captures the answers to those questions. By documenting instructional decisions, teachers will not have to reinvent the map every year, only refine it. The map is the viable curriculum or master learning plan.

Viable means living. It doesn't help to have a map if you never unfold it or to have a GPS if you never turn it on. The CAR curriculum is not a document that sits on a shelf or a website collecting dust. It is an essential tool that drives daily instruction and the conversations of the PLC. Ongoing engagement in the CAR conversations will cause the map to become an ever-evolving document that moves all students closer to the destination.

Curriculum is at the heart of the educational practice. If educators are to be held accountable for student growth, they should be confident that the curriculum they are asked to deliver is well-aligned with the standards students are expected to master. Can an educator be confident that the curriculum he/she had no part in developing or the textbook he/she is handed to use is well-aligned? In many cases, educators have little control over the district's curriculum.

The conversations presented in chapter 2 will guide the collaborative dialogue that allows PLCs to develop, implement, reflect on and continually revise and strengthen their curriculum based on current student data. The map will not only guide daily teacher practice but will become an invaluable tool for principals that results in far deeper conversations about practice than any review of lesson plans. The conversations will build professional confidence in the work of teaching, learning and leading. Educators will be able to ensure a tightly aligned equitable system of curriculum and instruction that will, in turn, ensure student growth. In order for this to occur, the curriculum must contain the next three components of CAR.

### *Standards and Aligned Student Learning Objectives*

The curriculum must be based on grade-level content area standards. Those standards must be unpacked into clear, specific, student-friendly learning objectives that every teacher in that grade level/content area uses as the objectives of their daily instruction. In some schools, a small group of educators is tapped to develop the curriculum document. If that document does not include the specific lesson objectives required to master the standards, then each teacher is left to their own interpretation of what the standard requires of the students. Or, what if the curriculum document is solely based on the textbook, which, by the way, the textbook publisher assures is aligned to the content and grade-level standards? Teachers can just follow the book and either develop their own lesson objectives or use the ones the publisher has provided. This makes it impossible to ensure that an equitable and aligned universal curriculum is delivered to every student.

### *Effective Instruction*

Curriculum must also detail the specific instructional strategies, activities, and resources that will help students achieve their learning goals. The textbook does not drive the instruction, the standards do. Textbooks and other materials are only resources. Following a textbook, as if it were the curriculum, is a detriment to a well-aligned map. A textbook might be taking you way off course. It is the job of the PLC to ensure that all activities and resources are aligned to agreed-upon learning objectives. Specific CAR conversations will drive the creation of this part of the map.

### *Formative and Summative Assessments*

Even if you have a good map, it is important to check and make sure you are moving in the right direction. Often, when someone gives you directions, they may tell you to look for guideposts along the way, the convenience store on the right, the bank on the left. Educators' guideposts are classroom formative and summative assessments built into their curriculum. Are we checking students' progress throughout an instructional unit to ensure they are headed toward mastery? If not, how do we get them back on the right road?

As schools prepared to welcome students back after the first wave of the pandemic, there was a lot of conversation about learning loss. Many experts warned of getting mired in a remediation mindset when what was needed was an acceleration of learning. In order to enable students to continue learning, schools needed a well-designed system of timely and targeted formative assessments that could be used throughout the year to identify gaps in prerequisite skills. Data from these classroom assessments were used to fill in gaps while learning progressed. This process necessitated that PLCs had the opportunity to collaboratively analyze data and collectively build appropriate differentiated lessons. Students in schools where educational leaders had already set up the structures for this work were at a distinct advantage.

In the CAR process, the creation of common formative and summative classroom assessment tools related to shared learning goals provides PLCs with the opportunity to engage in ongoing, authentic, timely and relevant data analysis that immediately drives the next steps in instruction.

The elements represented by the inside circles of the framework represent the CAR's common definition of the teaching and learning cycle—PLCs engaged in the continuous development, implementation, reflection on and revision of curriculum, instruction and assessment. The focus of PLC work does not change with every new initiative. The PLC has one goal—to continually adjust their practice in ways that are purposeful, data-driven and move the school ever closer to its shared destination.

## Culture—The Terrain

The culture of the school will determine whether educators and their students are traveling on smooth or rocky roads in order to reach the destination. Although it is one of the last components of CAR, it is certainly not the least. In fact, school culture is often the biggest barrier to the work of the PLC. Framing the outside of the process are the three components of school culture: the climate for learning, the degree of shared leadership, and the effective communication of connections.

The school culture is the result of the reinforcement of certain beliefs and values related to student learning, relationships, and leadership. The fact that these beliefs and values, whether spoken or unspoken, have existed for years, makes a change in culture difficult. But when challenging roadblock thinking a shift in the school culture is necessary and will determine the success and sustainability of the change.

CAR establishes a community of learners for both students and adults. Chapter 3 will examine the components of a collaborative professional climate. If PLCs are to work together to improve student learning, they must exist in a collegial environment that supports shared ownership, shared responsibility and shared leadership.

Chapter 4 will delve deeply into the structures necessary to create a positive and productive learning environment for students.

### *Shared Leadership*

Leadership is not a solo activity. Where top-down leadership is the norm, low staff morale often follows. Such morale is caused by a poor affective environment. It is sad when teachers have to be reminded that they most likely went through a rigorous hiring process. Their resumes were chosen, they were interviewed and someone made the decision that their skills, knowledge and abilities were exactly what were needed for the students in their school. Unfortunately, for some, once they are on the job, their opinions are not sought and their input into decisions is nil, even those decisions related to the core of their work—curriculum, instruction, and assessment. No longer feeling valued and able to make a contribution to the broader school community, they adopt the "my students" attitude resulting in negative feelings of frustration, apathy, and a sense of disconnectedness or isolation.

The CAR framework acknowledges the fact that principals and formal leaders alone cannot improve the quality of instruction, especially if the goal is to build the capacity to enhance instruction every day in every classroom. Strong individual teachers may be able to improve instruction in their own classrooms, but their impact will not be felt school wide. Only through collaboration, distributed leadership, mutual accountability, and shared decision-making can both formal leaders and teacher leaders collectively impact instruction across grade levels and content areas, turning a "my students" culture into an "our students" one.

The most effective formal leaders facilitate leadership in others and build the collective capacity for teaching, leading, and learning. Best results occur when formal leaders provide the time and structures for collaboration. Respecting and valuing teacher expertise, they allow teams to make decisions focused on curriculum, instruction and assessment and the message then becomes clear. Every teacher is an instructional leader. Everyone's contribution is essential in order for all students to have the same opportunity to reach their destination. Whether a teacher facilitates a PLC meeting, brings a valuable resource to the table, guides a data analysis session or develops an effective unit lesson, if they are positively impacting the work of their colleagues, they are leaders. Cultures that support shared leadership result in strong feelings of professionalism, optimism and collective efficacy.

The "I can't do one more thing syndrome" is taking a toll on schools everywhere. The continual piling on of initiatives, the urgency of meeting compliance deadlines and the constant switching of gears have led to higher levels of frustration and even anger when the "one more thing" they have to do is not seen as something that makes a difference for students. Michael Fullan and Joann Quinn note, "Overload, multiple initiatives, silos and compliance-driven mandates seem the norm." They go on to note that these forces generate "continuous churn" (Fullan and Quinn, 2016). CAR provides a way for school leaders to manage the churn and instead focus efforts on the elements of practice that will create continuous improvement. It provides leaders with a tool that enables them to continually communicate the purpose of any decisions and/or actions by showing how they contribute to strengthening what really matters—shared leadership for student learning within a collaborative culture that builds collective professional capacity to improve student outcomes.

Fullan and Quinn (2016) call on leaders to create coherence by defining the moral purpose, creating collaborative cultures, focusing on the teaching-learning nexus, and building the internal capacity of the organization through shared accountability. CAR is a coherence framework that provides a vision along with the tools and resources that help leaders operationalize and achieve that vision. The destination, student learning, establishes a clear direction. PLCs operate in a collaborative culture that ensures they remain focused on teaching and learning. As Hargreaves notes, "The challenge of coherence is not to clone or align everything so it looks the same in all schools. If we are all on the same page nobody is reading the entire book! The challenge, rather, is how to bring diverse people together to work skillfully and effectively for a common cause that lifts them up and has them moving in the same direction with an impact on learning, achievement, and results" (Hargreaves and Shirley, 2009, p. 95). Implementation of the CAR framework improves schools from within, building in shared accountability for reaching the destination. Throughout the process high expectations for students and the professionals who serve them also fuel the journey.

## The Drivers: Principal and Teacher Effectiveness

The current educator evaluation system is not designed for increasing educator effectiveness and building capacity, but rather for the purpose of accountability. As a result, the emphasis on teacher evaluation is misguided as it often assumes that by conducting a certain number of classroom observations the supervisor can assess the overall quality of a teacher's performance. Add to that the belief that standardized student achievement data will clearly identify who is effective and who is not. The use of evaluation frameworks is also meant to guide decisions about appropriate professional development opportunities for individual teachers. Sounds logical, however, let's look at this through a different lens.

Can we really improve all students' outcomes by focusing on snapshots of individual classroom practice? A principal may visit a teacher three times a year. They may hold a pre-conference to discuss the goals of the lesson to be viewed, ask the teacher to reflect on the lesson, write a post-observation report and meet the teacher to discuss the report. All of this focus is on one lesson, so what about the other lessons the teacher conducts in the course of the school year? Is the teacher reflecting on each of those lessons? Who is providing feedback? How is this process helping to ensure student growth and the refinement of teacher practice throughout the year?

CAR builds capacity for better teaching and improved learning in every classroom. Teachers become more effective when they work together to create and implement a viable curriculum, analyze data, and share best practices for improving student outcomes. The more PLC members and school leaders engage in the 10 conversations the more effective their practice becomes, thus creating a cycle of continuous schoolwide improvement of teaching and learning.

Remember the CAR process is about creating coherence to make sense of what we do. Evaluation should not be a compliance mandate, instead it should be viewed as just one part of a systemic growth process. If, indeed, the PLC conversations are targeted and focused on practice, teachers will, in fact, be addressing the indicators of their evaluation system, not just for three lessons out of the year, but for every lesson in every instructional unit throughout the year. Observations and pre- and post-conferences will be truly meaningful, as they are part of a year-long dialogue about teaching and learning.

The same idea holds true for the leader. Principal evaluation frameworks include several indicators related to instructional leadership. Effective leaders ensure a well-aligned curriculum is taught, assessment data is analyzed, and the analysis leads to changes in practice. Effective leaders also provide high-quality professional learning opportunities for all educators. Effective leaders create a culture of learning. CAR provides the process that makes those goals attainable.

## CLOSING

Clearly, CAR is a comprehensive framework. The purpose of this book is to assist leaders in strengthening the CAR components through an integrated process. Leaders cannot just focus on one component at a time. Throughout the book, it will become clear that actions taken in one area will either positively or negatively impact other areas. Subsequent chapters will enable the reader to explore and uncover the advantages of implementing the CAR framework in a way that honors the work of educators, children, and the community and builds an effective and logical structure to address positive change and growth. The next four chapters focus deeply on the central elements of instructional practice and school culture. Resources will be provided to help the reader shift focus from compliance and programs to process and practice in order to begin a coherent journey of continuous improvement.

## REFERENCES

Barth, R. (1991). *Improving schools from within.* San Francisco: Jossey Bass.

DuFour, R. (2004). What is a professional learning community? ASCD: Educational Leadership. Retrieved from https://www.ascd.org/el/articles/what-is-a-professional-learning-community.

DuFour, R., and Fullan, M. (2013). *Cultures that last.* Bloomington: Solution Tree.
Fullan, M. (2014). *The principal: three keys to maximizing impact.* San Francisco: Jossey Bass.
Fullan, M., and Quinn, J. (June 2016). *Coherence making.* Alexandria: The School Superintendents Association. Retrieved from https://my.aasa.org/AASA/Resources/SAMag/Jun16/Fullan.aspx.
Hargreaves, A. and Shirley, D. (2012). *The fourth way: The inspiring future for educational change*. Thousand Oaks: Corwin Press.

# *Chapter 2*

# Is Your GPS Working? Curriculum as the Master Learning Plan

> It is true that in today's current educational reality, teachers and administrators feel overwhelmed and inundated with change. It is because of this fact that professional dialogue is critical. A positive culture of collaboration is more essential now than ever. Unfortunately, however, unstructured "dialogue" or traditional meeting formats often do not lead to educational gains. The Connected Action Roadmap changes the conversation and focuses teachers on ways in which to keep the emphasis at all times on students and student achievement while removing the external barriers that often distract from personal and professional growth and development.
>
> —Kristin O'Neil, Superintendent, Lindenwold School District

Several years ago, the curriculum of Caroline L. Reutter School was in disarray. There was little evidence of data-informed instruction. Assessment dialogue only focused on data from mandated state tests. According to Principal Ted Peters, "Teachers were relying upon outdated 'best practices' that were woven into an outdated curriculum." Immediately, Ted formed a school leadership team and built PLCs supporting them with coaching and feedback, yet the PLCs were viewed by many teachers as another "administratively-driven task" that lacked purpose. With the introduction of CAR, Principal Peters writes that "our teacher leaders immediately grabbed hold of CAR and understood its important message and how it would help to organize the change process of our school." Within six months of implementing CAR, according to Peters, "our teacher leaders took over the facilitation role of their collaborative learning teams and dissected the curriculum. Over time they developed common summative assessments and common formative assessments. Data from these assessments drove immediate changes to the curriculum, as teams developed a true collaborative method of data analysis."

The story of Caroline L. Reutter School illustrates the power of the continuous cycle of improvement that is the heart of CAR. Redefining the work of PLCs, teachers engage in ten specific conversations to strengthen curriculum, instruction, and assessment. There are many different interpretations of the term, curriculum, the purpose it serves, and its connections to daily instruction.

When speaking with educators they often define curriculum as one of two things. The first is a document produced by the school district—the written curriculum. Often the interpretation of that document is left to each individual teacher, thus, the taught curriculum varies from classroom to classroom. Second, educators point to the textbook used to teach the content. If textbooks are viewed as the map, then implementation means following the manual and moving from one chapter to the next. The idea of the textbook or program as the curriculum has added to the outsourcing of practice and the loss of educator ownership for teaching and learning.

In this chapter, we will use a simple definition: *a curriculum is a common master learning plan for teaching the content area skills and knowledge that students need to learn at each grade level.* If our destination is higher levels of student learning, then educators must effectively and consistently use this master plan as our map or GPS. The GPS must provide clear direction to ensure that every educator can safely guide every student to the destination.

**Roadblock Thinking: If teachers use the curriculum documents created by a small group of teachers over the summer, they should be held responsible for ensuring student growth when students are assessed on grade-level standards.**

The small group of teachers selected to create the curriculum document have had a chance to discuss the standards and make decisions on how best to teach them. Once this document is given to other teachers to implement, those educators are at a disadvantage. They have not had the opportunity to fully understand how the design elements of the document align and why certain instructional decisions were made. By not participating in this process, they are left to interpret the master learning plan without the benefit of shared knowledge and shared understanding. If every teacher is responsible for student learning, then every teacher should be involved in creating the roadmap to get there. They need to have a deep and shared understanding of the standards and an opportunity to make sound instructional decisions for the students they teach. The only way they can ensure the curriculum they are using will meet the needs of the students is for them to take part in its development. In the CAR framework, developing a curriculum is not an event nor does it culminate in the production of a document or the use of a specific textbook.

The only way to ensure that there is a shared understanding of the master learning plan and that the plan is consistently implemented is to make the work of curriculum development and implementation an ongoing, reflective, and collaborative process—the work of the PLC.

The PLC is the vehicle that moves us toward higher levels of student learning. Like any vehicle the PLC needs fuel. As mentioned earlier, CAR provides ten specific conversations that PLCs need to have in order to create and implement their master plan for learning. An instructional unit template captures the results of the PLC conversations while promoting strong alignment between the key elements of an effective learning map—standards, instruction, and assessment. Together, the conversations and the template fuel a PLC process that supports the tight connection between teacher collaboration, curriculum, and classroom instruction.

**Forward Thinking: If every teacher is responsible for student growth, then every teacher needs to engage in developing, implementing, and revising a common master learning plan for the content and the students they teach. This will ensure that every teacher's practice is grounded in a viable curriculum marked by a tight alignment between grade-level standards, instruction, and the assessments that will be used to measure student growth.**

## CONNECTING CONVERSATIONS TO THE MASTER COMMON LEARNING PLAN

It is important to note the work of Grant Wiggins and Jay McTighe (1998) related to *Understanding by Design*. They established a powerful foundation for the creation of a meaningful curriculum. It is not the goal of this section to recreate that process nor demonstrate how to develop a "better" curriculum document. The purpose of this chapter is to illustrate how any curriculum document is only as effective as the professional collaboration that occurs in order to build educators' collective capacity to make that document come alive through effective classroom practice.

The 10 Conversations of CAR help close the gap between the written, the taught and the learned curriculum. Instead of creating documents that are rarely used in connection to daily lessons, the 10 PLC Conversations in Appendix B allow educators to constantly reflect on and revise the master learning plan in order to meet the needs of the students they currently serve.

The 10 conversations relate to areas of practice that have been the focus of many educational books and resources. Many educators have engaged in learning related to the standards they teach. Some have utilized backward design to create curriculum documents, and teachers know the importance of formative and summative assessment and data-driven instruction. These terms are neither novel nor revolutionary. Exactly! Remember the teaching and learning cycle in CAR is a process. It recognizes that teachers have many tools—their own knowledge and expertise, plentiful research and numerous professional resources that identify best practices. What teachers do not have is a continuous process for collaboratively using these tools to strengthen the key elements of practice, so that they result in an effective master learning plan for the students they serve.

The CAR process does not end with the development of the curriculum document. The process is never-ending! As new students arrive in classrooms and as new resources or innovative technology become available, educators continue to engage in the same process, the same ten conversations, continually revising and refining both their craft and the master learning plan. The goal is to collectively follow a map and when something takes you off course, adjust your route, so that all students eventually arrive at the destination. Engaging in these ten conversations is an essential part of the CAR journey.

**Roadblock Thinking: There is no problem if each teacher that teaches the same grade level and content creates their own learning objectives.**

Simply put, if each teacher translates the standards differently, how can educators be assured every student is engaged in instruction that aligns with the very standards that will be measured on the end of year assessment? If a teacher is engaging students in activities and assignments that are aligned to Student Learning Objectives (SLOs) that they have created, but those SLOs are not aligned to the standards, the students may very well be successful on those assignments, but that will not translate to success when they are measured on grade-level standards.

Second, if every teacher in a content area-/grade-level PLC is teaching to a different set of SLOs, how can they possibly engage in the collaborative analysis of student data to address gaps in achievement for all students? And how does that impact the ability to provide every student with equitable instruction?

**Forward Thinking: The creation of common SLOs is the foundation for equitable instruction. Common SLOs support the development of a common master learning plan and common assessments that lead to the effective collaborative analysis of student assessment data across a content area and grade level.**

## DEVELOPING THE MASTER LEARNING PLAN: CREATING A VIABLE CURRICULUM

### Conversation 1: Unpack Content Standards into Clear, Specific, Student-Friendly Learning Objectives

Content standards are statements of what we expect students to know, understand and be able to do. Unpacking the standards is a process used to analyze each standard and translate it into SLOs that will drive daily instruction. Often district curriculum documents contain the standards, but when creating their daily lesson plans, every teacher interprets each standard to create their own learning targets.

Unpacking the standards into clear, specific student-friendly learning outcomes is essential. PLCs utilize the unpacking worksheet using a four-step protocol to accomplish this task. The Unpacking a Standard worksheet can also be found in Appendix C. Figure 2.1 is an example of a team's use of the following four steps:

- Step One: Underline the nouns in the standard. The nouns in the standard define the "what" students must know and understand. Make sure to include clarifying adjectives that are key to understanding what the standard requires.
- Step Two: Circle the verbs. Make sure to include any clarifying adverbs that are key to understanding what the standard requires. The verbs identify what students should be able to do with the knowledge, skills, and understandings they develop. This is a key step as it enables teachers to clearly define the level of cognitive complexity required for the performance expectations that drive the creation of aligned assessments.
- Step Three: Create student-friendly learning objectives. Note that the examples use the acronym WALT which stands for We Are Learning To or We are Learning That.

## Unpacking a Standard

<table>
<tr><td colspan="2"><u>CCSS.ELA-LITERACY.W.2.1</u><br><br>Write opinion <u>pieces</u> in which they introduce the <u>topic</u> or <u>book</u> they are writing about, state an <u>opinion</u>, supply <u>reasons</u> that support the opinion, use linking <u>words</u> (e.g., because, and, also) to connect opinion and reasons, and provide a concluding <u>statement</u> or <u>section</u>.</td></tr>
<tr><td colspan="2">Knowledge/Concepts<br>What do students need to know/understand?<br><u>Underline</u> the nouns<br><br>List Nouns: PIECES, TOPIC, BOOK, OPINION, REASONS, WORDS, STATEMENT, SECTION</td></tr>
<tr><td>Skills<br><br>What do students need to be able to do?<br><u>Circle</u> the verbs<br><br>List Verbs: WRITE, INTRODUCE, STATE, SUPPLY, SUPPORT, USE, CONNECT, PROVIDE</td><td>Level of Complexity<br>(Circle the level)<br><br><u>Bloom's Taxonomy</u><br><br>Remember/Understand<br><br>Apply/Analyze<br><br>Evaluate/Create</td></tr>
<tr><td colspan="2">Student-Friendly Learning Objectives Aligned to this Standard<br><br>WALT INTRODUCE A TOPIC OR BOOK<br>WALT PROVIDE AN OPINION ABOUT THE TOPIC OR BOOK WE ARE WRITING ABOUT<br>WALT PROVIDE REASONS THAT SUPPORT THE OPINION<br>WALT USE LINKING WORDS (E.G., BECAUSE, AND, ALSO) TO CONNECT THE OPINION AND REASONS<br>WALT PROVIDE A CONCLUDING STATEMENT OR SECTION</td></tr>
</table>

**Figure 2.1 Sample: Unpacking a Standard.**

This phrase is used to emphasize the need for student-friendly language. Sharing learning targets in a language they can understand makes every student feel that they are an essential partner in the classroom collaborative learning team.

- Step Four: Identify the cognitive complexity of each verb using a classification system like Bloom's Taxonomy, Marzano's Taxonomy or Webb's Depth of Knowledge. It is important to do this in the context of the SLO. What level of thinking is required for mastery of each SLO? The verbs will inform the creation of formative and summative assessments. This step ensures that the SLOs are taught and assessed at the appropriate level of rigor.

## Conversation 2: Cluster the Standards and Student-Friendly Learning Objectives into Instructional Units

Conversation 2 focuses on grouping the standards and the aligned SLOs into several manageable instructional units that are the organizational framework for the common master learning plan. To accomplish this task, it is important to consider the relationships among the standards and the natural connection between them. When planning the unit, the PLC should consider the following questions:

1. How do groups of standards and SLOs relate to each other and support one another? Can they be grouped by topic, by skills or by themes?
2. Do certain standards and SLOs need to be placed in earlier units to build foundational skills and knowledge that will support learning in subsequent units?
3. Are there priority standards that should be placed in more than one unit so that students have multiple opportunities to apply key skills and concepts in a variety of learning experiences?

As this conversation unfolds, PLCs utilize the CAR Instructional Unit Template to capture their decisions. The template can be found in Appendix D. Although students will apply skills and knowledge from previous units, each unit should focus only on those standards and SLOs that will be explicitly taught and assessed in that unit. Placing too many standards and aligned SLOs in one unit detracts from the depth and clarity of what PLCs want students to know, understand or be able to do during a particular length of time.

The CAR process provides a vastly different approach to building and organizing curricula—one that focuses deeply on the process, dialogue, and collaboration. While most curriculum development approaches center around writing one unit at a time—from start to finish – before moving on to the next unit, the CAR approach relies on a macro perspective of the course during the initial phase. Teachers consider ALL of the standards for which they are responsible to teach and, after collaboratively unpacking the standards, they determine in which units the standards and SLOs will be placed. As they go through this process, they develop a deep understanding of the standards, a powerful professional learning experience in and of itself.

After completing conversations 1 and 2, each set of clustered standards should be placed in the standards section of the CAR Instructional Unit Template. The SLOs aligned to those standards should be placed in the SLO/WALT column on the template in the order in which they will be taught.

These CAR instructional units collectively lay out the shared master learning plan. Now the PLC is ready to continue the conversations and develop the instructional components of the first unit.

Figure 2.2 shows the direct connection between the CAR conversations and the Instructional Unit Plan Template. As you read the rest of the conversations look at where the results of the conversations are captured on the unit document. The CAR conversations lead to quality instructional decisions that directly impact daily instruction.

The Guide to Developing the CAR Instructional Unit Plan document found in Appendix E can be a helpful reference as teams move through these conversations. It

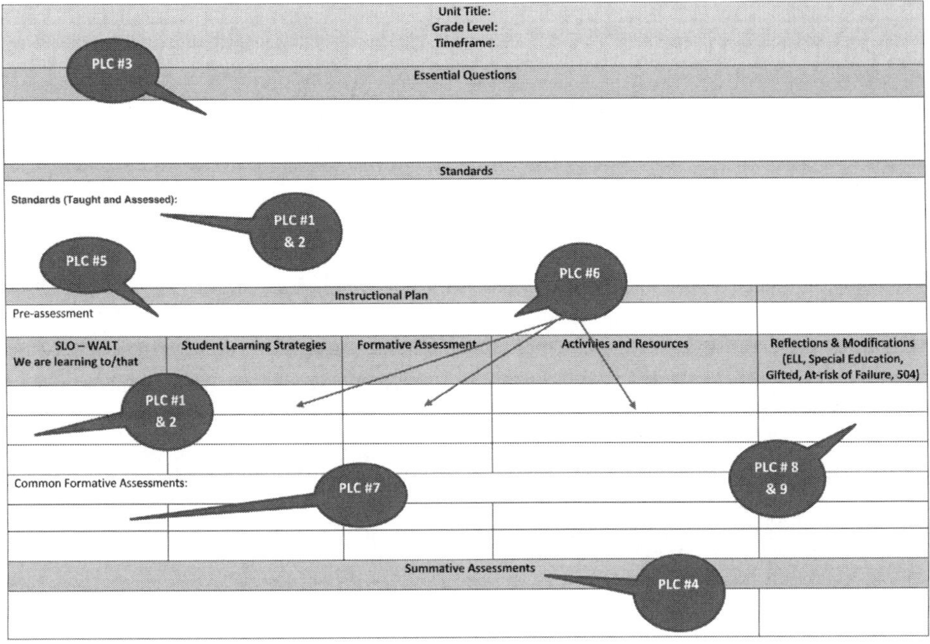


CAR © 2021

**Figure 2.2 CAR Unit Template with PLC Conversations.**

summarizes the content of each conversation and can also be instrumental in creating a common language related to the components of teaching and learning.

The teachers at Caroline L. Reutter School understood that these two conversations provided the basis for all of their work. By unpacking every standard, they arrived at a common understanding of its meaning and were able to effectively answer the question, "What do we want students to know, understand, and be able to do?" They also saw the benefit of using student-friendly language that would help ensure that their students clearly understood what they were learning. The collective understanding of the standards, SLOs and the sequence of instruction gave the educators at Caroline L. Reutter School a deep common focus that would drive their PLC conversations.

The CAR Instructional Unit Template is the foundational tool that is the bridge between the written, taught, and learned curriculum. Since the results of each of the ten conversations will be captured on this unit plan, PLCs do not need agendas or minutes. Their development work, their reflections and their revisions are all captured in this document. As teachers collaborate, their practice is strengthened, and the document is continually revised creating a cycle of continuous improvement of teaching and learning.

## Conversation 3: Create Essential Questions

The work of *Understanding by Design* (McTighe and Wiggins, 1998) laid the groundwork for developing instructional units in a way that ensures not only that teachers have a deep understanding of what they are teaching, but also that students have a deep understanding of what they are learning, It is important for students to not view learning as a discrete set of experiences—we master these SLOs, pass the test, and move to the next set of goals; or we use this knowledge and these skills in English Language Arts, but put them aside when the bell rings and we move to science class. Instead, students need to see their learning as a continuous journey, understanding that what they learn is connected and relevant to real-world ideas that transcend across units and content areas.

What are essential questions? As the PLCs unpack the standards and place them into the CAR Instructional Unit Template, conversations will naturally lead to seeing the emergence of big ideas. These big ideas, when changed into questions, promote critical thinking and help to make learning connections visible to students. Here are a few sample essential questions:

- Why is it important to support ideas with evidence?
- How can a quantity be represented in a variety of ways?
- How does punctuation affect meaning?
- How does the understanding of cultures help to build relationships?

As the PLCs develop essential questions, they should use the following questions adapted from *Essential Questions* (McTighe and Wiggins, 2013) to ensure that the questions will prompt students to be able to apply what they have learned in a broader context.

1. Is the question open-ended?
2. Does the question have more than one right answer?
3. Is the question in student-friendly language?
4. Does the question focus on key concepts taught in the unit?
5. Does the question require students to connect SLOs in order to see the bigger idea?
6. Does the question help students better understand why they are learning the content of the unit?
7. Does the question invite students to explore new ideas in relation to what they already know?
8. Can the question be used to uncover misconceptions in student thinking?
9. Can the question be used to assess students' learning throughout the unit?

Developing essential questions is not a requirement and should not become a compliance activity. Many curriculum developers have spent significant time developing essential questions to place in a curriculum document, but they rarely use them to enhance the learning process.

As the PLC considers whether they will develop and use essential questions within the units, they should discuss the following questions?

- How will the essential questions drive instruction within the unit or across a number of units?

- How can the questions connect the learning throughout the unit or across a number of units?
- How can they be used as an assessment tool to determine students' progress in grasping the application of the skills, knowledge and understandings addressed in a unit or across units?
- How can they foster cross-disciplinary connections?

## Conversation 4: Create Common Summative Assessments Including Rubrics, Exemplars and Non-exemplars

Summative assessments, also known as assessments *of* learning, are designed to measure student mastery of SLOs at the end of the instructional unit. Summative assessments evaluate how much students have learned and are used to assign a grade. Creating these assessments as a team allows all students to be measured against the same standard of performance. During the unpacking process, the PLCs created SLOs that clearly define what students should know, understand and be able to do. They also identified the level of thinking that students need to use to demonstrate their learning. This work now enables teachers to create aligned common summative assessments, as well as to define what mastery looks like. The following three questions can be used by PLCs to guide the development of end of unit assessments:

1. What type of assessment(s) will allow students to demonstrate mastery? Performance, written, portfolio? The PLC may use more than one assessment format to ensure they can evaluate all the learning goals in the unit. For example, the teachers may create a performance assessment and a multiple-choice or open-ended response test. Assessment types are determined by the level of thinking required by the standard.
2. How will the assessment be scored? What does mastery look like? This question should lead to the development of exemplars and rubrics to ensure consistent scoring of all students.
3. Review all the directions and questions from the students' perspective. Are there any areas that are unclear or that may cause possible confusion?

## Conversation 5: Design Pre-assessment and Use Data to Inform Instructional Decisions

As a result of the pandemic, the term accelerated learning has been used frequently to refer to the need to close learning gaps caused by extended school closures. The CAR framework embeds the process of accelerated learning into the teaching and learning cycle through the consistent use of formative assessments that will allow teachers to consistently identify and address the learning needs of each student as they move ahead with grade-level instruction. Accelerated learning is not a new process, it is an integral part of the curriculum, instruction, and assessment nexus. Educators must constantly assess and differentiate based on the needs of their students. The consequence of not doing so effectively only widens any existing achievement gap.

Pre-assessment design begins with identifying prerequisite skills that are essential for success in the unit. It can also be helpful to measure requisite knowledge and skills to determine if students have already mastered the content or have misconceptions that may be barriers to their learning. PLCs can determine the pre-assessment format ensuring careful alignment with the SLOs they intend to measure.

Before beginning a unit of instruction, the PLC should consider where students are in the learning cycle. In the formative assessment process, the pre-assessment of student knowledge and skills, thus, becomes critical in thinking about adjusting the path individual students will follow to master the unit SLOs. Pre-assessment will only be effective if the teachers are recording and collectively analyzing data related to each student's mastery of prerequisite and requisite skills and concepts. The PLC will then be able to develop unit activities, strategies and interventions to meet the needs of individual students throughout the unit. Pre-assessment is the first step in ensuring the common master plan addresses the varying needs of students. Teams can use the following questions when analyzing pre-assessment data to inform Conversation 6.

1. Which students in each class need to work on prerequisite skills and concepts? What skills? What concepts? What does this mean for unit planning? How will we address these gaps?
2. What misconceptions are evident in student responses?
3. Which students in each class have mastered the requisite skills? What skills? What does this mean for unit planning? What types of extension activities need to be developed?
4. What learning goals do we need to focus on during whole group instruction?
5. Is the pre-assessment effectively measuring student mastery of the prerequisites and requisites? Does it need revisions? Are the questions and/or tasks aligned to the SLOs? Are the directions clear?

### Conversation 6: Design Learning Experiences Including Instructional Activities, Student Strategies and Formative Assessments

Designing learning experiences is at the heart of what teachers do on a daily basis. Through the CAR process, this conversation intentionally leverages the knowledge and experience of the PLC as they create learning experiences directly related to each of the SLOs within a unit. Alignment of the instructional activities, resources, student strategies and formative assessments is essential. If you look at the components of this conversation and think—"this feels a lot like lesson planning"—you're right! However, instead of daily lesson planning, the CAR process guides PLCs to develop instructional units through which a single SLO or a group of SLOs might take one or several days to teach depending on the students. In that way, we define each of the instructional activities, materials, strategies, and formative assessments used to teach the SLO or a group of SLOs as a learning experience. Let's take a look at these components.

As PLCs discuss the SLOs for each unit, they consider which activities—instructional models and teaching strategies—are most effective to meet these learning outcomes. In doing this they also consider the learning needs of the students in their classrooms. For example, if an SLO calls for students to understand a specific concept, such as photosynthesis, the team would consider teaching models that support conceptual understanding such as the Concept Attainment Strategy or the Frayer Model. Similarly, the team would consider resources—materials, visuals, online tools, supplies—that also support the SLOs and the needs of the students. All too often, districts invest large sums of money in textbooks and programs without considering precisely how the information in the textbook/program directly connects to the students' ability to achieve the targeted SLOs. It is the standards and SLOs that drive the curriculum, not the other way around.

To explicitly build the independence of learners, the PLC is highly intentional in identifying student learning strategies that are aligned to the SLOs and are developmentally appropriate. A student learning strategy is an approach or a set of steps that students can use to independently engage in their own learning and successfully meet the SLO. Some of these strategies are content specific, such as the R.A.C.E. writing strategy or the CUBE math problem-solving strategy, and others are general, such as note-taking or active listening strategies.

While teachers should explicitly teach and model student learning strategies, they are quite different from instructional models discussed earlier. The goal is for students to use these learning strategies independently to support their own learning and apply what they have learned. Creating these strategies so that they are consistent across grade levels and content areas allows students to take responsibility for their learning by consistently employing the strategies they have been taught.

It is virtually impossible to design an impactful learning experience without developing formative assessments to guide instructional decisions. Unlike summative assessments, formative assessments occur throughout the unit and are designed to provide feedback to both the teacher and the student. Through this ongoing process, students and teachers focus directly on the SLOs in order to take stock of where the students' current work is in relation to the goal. Examples of formative assessments include:

- Temperature Gauges—immediate, in-the-moment assessments that give a sense of current student status and allow the teacher to adjust the pace or modify the content;
- Break Points—quick assessments at strategic points that allow the teacher to step back and revise the next steps in instruction
- Student-Directed Assessments—Peer and self-assessments that give both the student and teacher insight related to individual progress toward mastery of learning goals

At the end of the day, however, formatively assessing students is not the key—using the feedback from formative assessments is key. High-quality feedback is timely, constructive, specific, usable, and directly linked to the SLOs. The students use the feedback to reflect on and make adjustments to their learning. This encourages students to become more engaged and independent learners. Teachers use the feedback to reflect on and make adjustments to their teaching. As Robyn Jackson states,

> It is one thing to collect feedback about students' progress, but if you simply collect this feedbacks and never use it to adjust your instruction, then you are collecting it in vain. The data you receive from grading your assignments and assessments will give you feedback about the effectiveness of your own instruction. (Jackson, 2009, p.132)

Conversation 6 with its focus on designing the learning experience truly represents the art of teaching. As PLCs share their expertise and knowledge of activities, resources, student strategies and formative assessments aligned to the unit's SLOs, team members are able to implement those that will have the highest yield for the students in their classrooms. Rather than teachers independently working on daily lesson plans, the PLC works together to create a flexible and robust instructional unit. The common language established by the components of the instructional unit plan allows for deeper conversations about teaching and learning throughout the school community.

**Roadblock Thinking: The review of individual weekly lesson plans by principals or supervisors ensures that all the components of the instructional plan are aligned to the standards.**

Checking lesson plans has become a compliance-driven activity. When creating daily lesson plans, many teachers are required to include a reference to the standard if that ensures alignment. If supervisors want to ensure that standards-based instruction is being taught in every classroom they would have to spend a significant amount of time determining if the SLOs are aligned to the referenced standard and then determining if each lesson plan component is aligned to the SLO(s). Imagine the time such a review would require!

The use of weekly lesson plans also does not support effective practice. After teaching a lesson, if teachers find the students lack understanding of the skill or concept, the plan must be adjusted for the following day. Instructional Unit Plans allow PLCs to consistently adjust instruction based on student needs.

**Forward Thinking: Instructional Unit planning allows teachers to view the current learning in the context of the entire master learning plan.**

As the PLC revises and refines the plan based on student data they are continually adding to the repertoire of successful strategies and resources available for the varied learners in their classrooms. Because the unit plan is constructed horizontally, it allows both the teacher, and the supervisor that is monitoring instruction, to focus more clearly on alignment. The supervisor can also see how data analysis results in changes in the unit design. Discussion about these changes provides rich opportunities to strengthen the dialogue about teaching and learning between teachers and administrators.

## Conversation 7: Create Common Formative Benchmark Assessment Tools for Key Points Within the Unit of Study

Formative assessment is a driving force of teaching and learning throughout the unit of study. Common formative benchmark assessments that are administered at key points across the common master learning plan ensure that the PLC is providing all students with a differentiated learning experience that will ultimately allow them to achieve the unit SLOs. However, all too often, benchmark assessments have been defined and, in turn, utilized by educators in multiple ways. Unfortunately, this has led to various misinterpretations, misconceptions, and misuses of benchmark assessment data among teachers, administrators, parents, and students. For example, many schools use commercially developed benchmark assessments periodically throughout the school year. If these assessments are not aligned to the SLOs and/or if the data is not provided in a timely way to allow teachers to adjust instruction immediately, the analysis of that data is less likely to have an impact on addressing the needs of individual students.

To be clear, in the context of CAR, common formative benchmark assessments are developed by the PLC to assess progress toward mastery of a group of SLOs that have already been taught. They are not intended to derive a letter grade that evaluates performance. Instead, well-constructed common formative benchmark assessments are strategically designed to provide clear and targeted feedback to both teachers and students, promote effectively aligned instructional decisions and, ultimately, guide and advance individual student progress toward attainment of unit SLOs by the end of the instructional unit. Common formative benchmark assessments can be best described as assessments *for* learning.

Consistent with Conversation 4, creating common formative assessment tools as a team allows all students to be measured against the same standard of performance at key learning milestones throughout the unit experience. PLCs should consider the following questions to guide the development of their common formative assessment system:

1. What SLOs will be assessed?
2. What type of assessment will allow students to demonstrate mastery? Assessment types are determined by the level of thinking required by the standard.
3. How will the assessment be scored? What does mastery look like? This question should lead to the development of exemplars and rubrics to ensure consistent scoring of all students.
4. Review all the directions and questions from the students' perspective. Are there any areas that are unclear or that may cause possible confusion?

**Roadblock Thinking: If school teams and administrators review data from the classroom, district, and/or state assessments, they are engaged in data-driven instruction.**

Data-driven instruction has become a buzz phrase that has resulted in teachers spending endless hours examining the results of state assessments and commercial benchmark assessments that are a component of a district-wide plan to monitor student learning. The question remains, how is the analysis of this data actually driving changes in instructional practice? How is the data used in a timely way to impact the students that are currently sitting in each teacher's classroom? Although these assessments may provide some information related to students' proficiency in relation to the standards, they often lack detail about student performance in relation to specific skills and concepts related to those standards.

The CAR process engages PLCs in the use of data-driven learning. Teams analyze commonly developed formative and summative assessments that are aligned to the

SLOs that make up each unit of study. By formatively assessing student performance related to the SLOs throughout the unit, teachers and students can make adjustments and address gaps in learning before the summative assessment is given. Although the summative assessment is used to evaluate performance, the data should also be used formatively to continue to drive changes in instructional practice and address student learning needs.

**Forward Thinking: Teacher-developed common formative and summative assessments provide immediate actionable data in relation to standards-aligned SLOs. Data-driven learning allows both teachers and students to utilize assessment feedback to make adjustments to the teaching and learning process. When data is collaboratively analyzed, teachers can utilize guiding questions to examine their practice and build on one another's strengths to better address student learning needs.**

It is important to note that sharing assessment data can feel risky for teachers. It is a good idea to set some ground rules. Teachers should agree to be honest about what the data is showing. When reviewing data, the team must commit to not only looking at the performance of each class as a whole, but to examining each individual student's progress in meeting the unit SLOs. Teachers should avoid assigning blame for the outcomes to factors outside the classroom; for example, "If she only studied more" or "if only his parents would make sure he did his homework."

Since teachers sometimes feel vulnerable to judgment when they share their assessment results, leadership needs to send the message that formative data is not evaluative. The data should be used to focus, not on individual teachers, but on the needs of the students. The data is not a judgment about the teachers' instructional expertise, but evidence of what students learned. It should lead to a willingness to make changes in teacher practice. By working together and openly sharing instructional practices that worked and those that didn't, the team builds a collective capacity to improve every student's learning.

## Conversation 8: Analyze Formative Assessment Data throughout the Unit to Drive Instructional Planning, Differentiated Activities and Timely Interventions

Common formative benchmark assessments administered at key points throughout a unit allow the PLC to provide invaluable data to help teachers decide how to proceed with the learning journey. They may need to stop and adjust the route to ensure students are provided with the necessary differentiated instruction that will allow them to successfully arrive at the destination. PLCs can use the 4Rs, determining if each student is Ready to move on, needs Reinforcement in certain skills and concepts, needs targeted Reteaching or needs to be challenged with Reach activities. The information allows teachers to plan for flexible grouping. The PLC can share the workload with one teacher planning a Reteaching lesson while another plans the extension or Reach activity. It is important to remember that students should be provided feedback on their assessment results, and should be reassessed after any intervention to determine the next steps. When initial interventions are not successful, more intensive interventions may be required.

The CAR conversations support a tiered system of support. The units provide a universal, equitable curriculum for every student—Tier 1. The effective use of formative data allows for targeted intervention in the classroom through flexible grouping and differentiation—Tier 2. Tier 3 calls for more intensive intervention where instruction may be provided outside the classroom. However, when formative data is used effectively, it allows teachers to determine exactly what SLOs need to be the target of such instruction. It also enables classroom teachers to share the intervention strategies used at the Tier 2 level to further inform instruction at Tier 3. Ongoing and consistent progress monitoring is an essential component of any effective tiered system of support.

The best formative assessment system ensures that students also benefit from the data it generates. As such, the PLC explores ways to effectively utilize this data to provide timely, constructive, specific, usable feedback that is directly linked to the SLOs. Furthermore, PLC members equip their students with the ability to use the feedback to reflect on, make adjustments to, and take ownership of their own learning.

Common benchmark assessment data can also be used by the PLC to improve the unit design. For example, if several students struggled with an SLO, perhaps the PLC will want to adjust instruction in that area—build a new student strategy or find a different instructional resource.

PLCs should consider the following questions to guide the analysis of the data:

1. With which SLOs are most students struggling? What do their responses tell us about their misconceptions or misunderstandings?
2. What reteaching strategies and activities will be used with these students?
3. With which SLOs are students most successful? What do their responses tell us?
4. Which students need reinforcement or reach activities?
5. What strategies and activities will we develop for those students?
6. What additional instructional resources do we need to meet the learning needs of our students?
7. What does the data tell us about our instruction? What needs to change? What can we learn from one another?
8. How can the data be shared with students to encourage reflection, goal setting and ownership for learning?
9. Is the common formative benchmark assessment effectively measuring student achievement of the standards? Does it need revisions? Are the questions and/or tasks aligned to the SLOs? Are the directions clear?

Unit design is an evolving process. As PLCs grapple with these questions, develop differentiated lessons and refine unit instructional practices their work is captured in the unit template. The CAR conversations are constantly ensuring that the master plan or GPS keeps students on the path to learning.

### Conversation 9: Analyze Summative Assessment Data to Evaluate Student Progress, Revise Unit Learning Experiences, Revise Unit Assessments and Seek Targeted Professional Learning

Summative assessments are used to evaluate or grade student progress toward mastery of the standards at the end of the instructional unit. However, this data should also be used formatively. If the skills and concepts assessed are prerequisites for subsequent units, data can inform the PLCs planning for those units. In addition, opportunities for vertical articulation and sharing of summative data will provide information on prerequisite skills and concepts that will require further reinforcement in the following year.

Conversation 9 is also essential to unit revision. It will provide information on what activities, strategies and assessments need to be revised. Again, by examining what worked and what didn't, teams continually strengthen instruction for all students. Summative assessment data should also highlight areas for teacher growth through professional learning. While quality professional learning occurs routinely through the conversations, data analysis may lead the team to explore professional resources or attend targeted workshops that will help address a student learning issue uncovered by the data. Districts often find it difficult to demonstrate how professional learning impacts student learning. In the CAR process, there is a direct correlation. When a member of PLC attends a professional learning session and brings back information to the team and they use that information to make changes in practice, those changes can be seen in the instructional unit and their effectiveness can be determined using student data.

PLCs should consider the following questions to guide the analysis of the data:

1. With which SLOs are most students struggling? What do their responses tell us about their misconceptions or misunderstandings?
2. With which SLOs are students most successful? What do their responses tell us?
3. What interventions were used throughout the unit with the students who were struggling on the common formative assessment(s)? Did those students continue to make the same errors?
4. Will these SLOs be addressed again? In what unit? How will we strengthen that unit to reinforce skills and concepts for specific students? Are these SLOs prerequisite skills for future units? Which ones? How will we differentiate instruction in those units to support individual students?
5. What other teachers need this information?
6. What does the data tell us about our instruction? What needs to change? What can we learn from one another?
7. What professional resources or professional learning opportunities do we need to assist us in strengthening this instructional unit?
8. Is the summative assessment effectively measuring student mastery of standards? Does it need revisions? Are questions and tasks aligned to the SLOs? Are directions clear?

Collaborative analysis of data from common formative and summative classroom assessments is only powerful when the feedback from that analysis is used by students to adjust their learning and teachers to make changes in their instructional practice. Conversations 8 and 9 ensure that the master learning plan is responsive to students. The instructional units are never complete, never just put on a shelf. They are directly connected to classroom instruction and assessment. Appendix F provides a summary of the Important Role of Classroom Assessments and Common Assessments. Changes in the instructional units are the result of the PLC's continuous reflection on their practice through the lens of student learning outcomes—true data-driven instruction.

### Conversation 10: Discuss Grading Philosophy, Policies, and Procedures

"Grading seems to be regarded as the last frontier of individual teacher discretion. The same school leaders and community members who would be indignant if sports referees were inconsistent in their rulings continue to tolerate inconsistencies that have devastating effects on student achievement" (Reeves, 2009, p. 86). Although this conversation is the last, it actually occurs throughout unit development and assessment design. It begins when teachers identify the common SLOs and determine the evidence of mastery. It continues as common assessments, exemplars and rubrics are collaboratively developed. Many schools, after engaging in the previous CAR conversations, recognize the power of standards-based grading. They come to the conclusion that the goal of grading students is to evaluate their performance in relation to the standards.

At Caroline L. Reutter School, conversations 1 and 2 became the driving force in moving to standards-based grading. Teachers quickly realized that their experience of unpacking the standards had provided the necessary foundation. Having developed common instructional units with a common sequence of learning progressions, they were able to clearly communicate to both students and parents exactly what standards were the focus of each grading period. This helped the entire school community transition more smoothly from a traditional grading system to a proficiency-based model.

Adopting the philosophy of standards-based grading requires several shifts in thinking. A key question is, "What is the purpose of grading?" Teachers may have previously graded formative assessments rather than using them as tools for providing feedback and adjusting practice. Sometimes that was done to meet some arbitrary policy about how many grades must be logged in the grade book. They may also have developed their own systems for averaging grades, dealing with late assignments, or bestowing extra credit points. Some teachers may have assigned zeros to missing work, believing it is important to teach students to be responsible, while others gave students the opportunity to make up for missing work. In some instances, grades are also used to reflect effort, attitude, or work ethic.

Imagine the inequity that results when grading decisions are made by individual teachers. It then becomes possible for students' grades to be determined, not by their level of mastery of common standards, but by their placement in one teacher's class or another's. Grading conversations can be difficult, but PLCs must engage in this conversation to ensure grading practices are fair and equitable and that every student has the opportunity to be successful.

## THE CAR CONVERSATIONS—FUELING THE TRANSFORMATION OF PROFESSIONAL PRACTICE

For the last five years, the collaborative learning teams of Caroline L. Reutter School have engaged in the conversations outlined in this chapter. Principal Ted Peters often reflects that "nothing in our school is stationary." Teams are constantly analyzing the instructional units and assessments to identify areas of need and growth. Groups of teachers have grown into "fully collaborative learning teams that provide equitable instruction to all learners through a shared curriculum, common assessments and colleagues working together on shared methods of instruction." The shift from administrator-driven groups to authentic PLCs focused on the right work was evident when Peters overheard a conversation between two teachers in which one asked the other for help with a specific instructional strategy after the team analyzed common summative assessment data. Building the capacity of educators, strengthening teacher practice and engaging in a continuous cycle of school improvement grounded in collaboration and shared leadership is the most effective path to improving student learning.

## CLOSING

The shift from roadblock thinking to forward thinking organically takes place as a common vision, shared understanding, and an unwavering focus on the destination of student learning guides the work of all educators in the school building. The CAR conversations outlined in this chapter empower PLCs to embrace their role in the teaching and learning cycle. "Successful and sustainable improvement can never be done *to or even for teachers* it can only ever be achieved *by and with them*" (Hargreaves and Fullan, 2012, p. 45). As educators work together, they create a collegial climate that fosters true collective efficacy. Remember, the school's climate and culture can be the biggest barrier to effective professional collaboration and student learning. Attention must be given to establishing a professional learning environment that supports PLC work. The climate for adult learning is the focus of chapter 3.

## REFERENCES

Hargreaves, A., and Fullan, M. (2012). *Professional capital: Transforming teaching in every school.* New York: Teachers College Press.

Jackson, R. (2009). *Never work harder than your students and other principles of great teaching. Alexandria: Association for Supervision and Curriculum.* Alexandria: Association for Supervision and Curriculum.

McTighe, J. and Wiggins, G. (2013). *Essential questions: Opening doors to student understanding.* Alexandria: Association for Supervision and Curriculum.

Reeves, D. (2009). *Leading change in your school: How to conquer myths, build commitment and get results.* Alexandria: Association for Supervision and Curriculum.

Wiggins, G., and McTighe, J. (1998). *Understanding by design.* Alexandria: Association for Supervision and Curriculum.

## *Chapter 3*

# Supporting a Culture of Collaboration

> Our staff was very congenial before CAR, but not necessarily collegial. CAR changes that. After more than 4 years with CAR, our staff has meaningful PLCs at least once a week, where we discuss student learning, assessment data and instructional practices. These conversations spill over into our lunchtime chitchat, our hallway check-ins and our parking lot catch-ups.
>
> —Alicia Carney, Teacher Leader, Englewood Public Schools

The 10 PLC Conversations provide the focus for PLC teams, but they must take place in a work environment characterized by trust, respect, and a collective commitment. Think about the professional climate for educators using the following four descriptions:

- Civil: In a civil climate, adults fail to consistently demonstrate strong interpersonal skills and have limited opportunities for engagement with one another. Staff members are usually very focused on their individual work and their own job responsibilities and are somewhat disconnected from the larger school community. In a civil climate, educators would be lucky if someone greeted them as they walked down the hall in the morning.
- Congenial: In a congenial climate, adults demonstrate positive social relationship skills. They greet one another, eat lunch together, and share information about personal experiences. There is usually food involved in this "friendly" climate. The phrase, "We all get along," is often used to describe this environment.
- Contrived Collegial: In a contrived collegial environment, professionals are "forced" to work collaboratively often to fulfill a compliance requirement. Such a climate is usually top-down with administrators assigning work to teams. Contrived collegial environments often produce resentment due to professionals viewing their teamwork as a "waste of time." Professional Learning Community teams operating in a contrived collegial climate are in name only and do not function with a structure that supports teamwork focused on the common goal of student learning.
- Collegial: In a collegial climate, professionals are committed to working together to ensure that all students learn. Collegial climates are marked by mutual respect, a

shared mission, shared leadership and time for authentic collaboration, professional discourse, and job-embedded professional learning.

## AUTHENTIC COLLABORATION AND PROFESSIONAL DISCOURSE

Because CAR is a systemic approach to school improvement that focuses on the connections between the parts of the CAR framework, actions taken to strengthen one component will also strengthen other components. It is also important to recognize that when leaders provide the time and structures to engage in the CAR conversations, they are also strengthening the overall climate for learning. Neglecting this connection is another example of roadblock thinking.

**Roadblock Thinking: PLC practices have little impact on school climate. Educators often focus on the school climate for students, paying less attention to the collegial climate that makes optimal student and adult learning possible. Yet, research clearly shows a connection between professional learning and teacher morale.**

PLC practices, such as examining student work, analyzing student data, developing standards-based lessons, and creating common assessments, have a positive correlation with high levels of teacher morale. In turn, lower teacher morale correlates with PLC experiences focused on building issues, student behavior, and organizing grade-level events. In schools where PLCs operate in name only, resentment builds over the ineffective use of time, feelings of being treated unprofessionally grow and educator morale drops.

**Forward Thinking: Educators engaged in authentic collaboration related to student learning develop collective efficacy which in turn supports a positive climate for both student and adult learners.**

As Hargreaves notes,

> Professional learning communities, collaboration and change in general are as much about pulling people toward interesting change by the excitement of the process, the inspirational feeling of engagement, the connection to people's passions and purposes, the provision of time that is not consumed by classroom responsibilities or mandated change agendas, and the creation of not just a spreadsheet of higher test scores but also a culture of engaged and a successful learners. (Hargreaves and Fullan, 2012, p. 130)

The analysis of the research studies on teacher collegiality clearly identifies effective collaboration as a vital source of enhancement in staff professional growth, student learning and organizational effectiveness (Shah, 2012). By engaging in the CAR conversations, as outlined in chapter 2, teams experience shared ownership and accountability for the teaching and learning process. The process ignites their passion through a shared purpose.

Thus, collective teacher efficacy is the *number one* factor influencing student achievement (Hattie, 2016). A strong sense of collective efficacy, in turn, supports the development of a collegial climate. Educators realize that by working together they have the power to better meet the needs of all students. No longer existing in silos, their sense of confidence and professionalism blossoms.

The remainder of this chapter will focus on other key factors that support the collegial climate necessary to build collective efficacy.

## PROFESSIONAL EXPECTATIONS

Just as clear expectations for student behavior are an essential component of a positive climate for students, educators need to come to a consensus on what they expect from one another as professional colleagues. Issues between adult colleagues are often ignored or swept under the carpet with little understanding of how these conflicts impact the overall ability of professionals to collaborate with a focus on student learning. Although schools and educators set school and classroom expectations for student behavior, educators do not generally discuss their expectations of one another in an open and honest manner.

It is essential for all staff to have an open conversation that results in an agreed-upon list of expectations. School faculty can utilize the following simple protocol to engage all staff in developing their professional expectations:

1. Ask each staff member to create an individual list in response to the following question, "What do you expect from another as professional colleagues?"
2. Break into small groups and come to consensus on one list.
3. Post all the groups' lists and, as a staff, come to consensus on one list of expectations.

Appendix G shows an example of the professional expectations developed at one school.

In order to help educators be more specific about the behaviors that will enable them to meet their shared expectations it is helpful to discuss what each expectation requires colleagues to stop doing, continue doing or start doing when it comes to professional behavior. This ensures that everyone clearly understands the explicit behaviors that support the expectations.

Now the hard work begins. The last expectation on any list must state that everyone will hold each other accountable for agreed-upon expectations.

### Roadblock Thinking: Addressing negative adult behavior will only cause more problems.

This type of thinking prevents adults from openly addressing issues that are getting in the way of the school's efforts to build collective efficacy and maintain a focus on student learning. When negative behaviors are not addressed, they can take on a life of their own. With no way to effectively confront the behavior, educators often find themselves frustrated and take to airing their concerns with others in the teachers' lounge or parking lot. Left unchecked, such behaviors become ingrained in the culture.

**Forward Thinking: By holding each other accountable for agreed-upon expectations in positive and assertive ways, educators reinforce the types of behaviors that will lead to a productive and collaborative professional learning environment.**

The first step in deciding acceptable ways to hold each other accountable is to agree on the definition of accountability. Accountability is not about blaming or making someone apologize for their behavior. Accountability is a way to ensure follow-through on a commitment.

When someone does not live up to an agreed-upon expectation, does the staff give each other permission to speak up, not as an attack, but in a way that provides a gentle reminder of why the expectation is important to the collective work? Has everyone agreed that such reminders are not personal but relate to the ability to meet our common goal? Do we agree to first assume positive intent? Have we clearly articulated that by holding ourselves and one another accountable we are building a positive work culture?

It is imperative to collectively engage in these conversations so that adults create a safe space where mutual accountability is more than a buzzword. Over time, the focus on student learning and the results it brings strengthens the shared commitment to professional expectations and these expectations become part of the culture of the school.

Norms are another set of commitments that are made by each PLC team. Agreed-upon meeting norms can be developed by the team by allowing everyone to respond to the question, "What agreements will help us to make the most efficient use of our team time? What will prevent us from collaborating fully to achieve our common goals?" The following is a sample list of meeting norms:

## MEETING NORMS

1. Be honest about your current reality.
2. Actively listen and participate.
3. Voice and respond to concerns positively and non-judgmentally.
4. Be respectful.
5. Show professional responsibility.
    - Be on time to meetings
    - Be prepared for meetings
    - Complete tasks in a timely manner
6. Slow down to think, reflect, and puzzle about things.
7. Hold each other accountable for agreed-upon norms.

Notice that the last norm speaks to accountability. The team should agree on the best ways to address any lapse in adhering to the norms. Norms should also be revisited periodically to decide how well they are working and suggest any need for additions or revisions. Appendixes H and I provide both a group reflection tool and an individual reflection tool that PLC members can utilize to assess their adherence to the norms.

## ALIGNED EXPECTATIONS FOR STAFF AND STUDENTS

**Roadblock Thinking: There needs to be little alignment between the expectations for students and the expectations for adults.**

Setting clear expectations for student behavior is certainly important. As previously discussed, professional expectations are also essential. Moreover, it is critical that these two sets of expectations align. Adult modeling of appropriate social and emotional learning skills supports students in mastering these skills. Consider the following example:

> Teacher A arrives several minutes late to relieve Teacher B on cafeteria duty. Teacher B is clearly frustrated and remarks, "Great, now I have a shorter time to eat!" Teacher A walks away and teacher B is overheard grumbling about Teacher A's tardiness in an angry tone.

Students who overhear this exchange may very well think, "Do as I say, not as I do." So much for respect and solving problems peacefully. Now consider how this same scenario could have modeled mutual respect and the use of conflict resolution skills that have been taught to students in the school in order to build more positive relationships.

> Teacher A arrives several minutes late to relieve teacher B on cafeteria duty. Teacher B uses an I message to communicate her frustration, "I feel very frustrated that you were not able to be on time. Please try to arrive on time tomorrow." Teacher A responds, "I felt so much pressure when I knew I'd be late. I was unable to get here on time due to an incident in my classroom. I will do my best to be on time from here on and if there is an emergency, I will notify the office to send coverage."
>
> Teacher B responds, "Good idea. I think we should let the office know that we need to develop a plan when emergencies arise. Thanks."

The actions of Teacher B in the first scenario tear at the fabric of a positive collegial climate. In the latter example, Teacher A and Teacher B engage in conflict resolution, reinforcing how this process can work for students in order to maintain healthier relationships.

**Forward Thinking: Ensuring that expectations for students and adults are aligned supports students in building strong social and emotional learning skills.**

The school staff should review the expectations they have set for students and the social and emotional learning skills that are taught to support better relationships. Consider ways adults can better model these behaviors.

## A SHARED MISSION

**Roadblock Thinking: There is little connection between a shared mission or vision, educator practice, and a collegial climate.**

Most schools have developed some sort of mission or vision statement. School leaders know that vision setting is necessary, but often fail to make that vision come alive through consistent action and reflection. How can schools ensure that a common mission is more than words on paper? How can it actually drive necessary changes in their organizational structures and educational practices? Consider this sample mission statement:

## MISSION STATEMENT

We function as a cooperative unit of dedicated teachers to create a positive, child-centered environment that fosters respect, responsibility, lifelong learning, and success for all students.

This may hang in the foyer of any school as a way to communicate the school community's commitment to its students. However, such a mission statement fails to articulate the actions that will be necessary to achieve "success for all students."

**Forward Thinking: A collaboratively developed student-focused mission statement built on shared beliefs and values is essential to creating a collaborative culture that strives to meet that mission daily.**

Now refer to the mission statement in Appendix J. This second statement is actually from the same school as the first, only three years after a new principal arrived. Let's consider the actions the school staff engaged in to develop a mission statement that could inspire and unify the school community.

Notice that the mission is built on beliefs and values. Creating consensus around shared beliefs and values took time. As the CAR process was implemented, the school staff consistently reflected on the question, "What do we now believe and what do we now value that will move us closer to achieving our collective mission?"

As new practices such as a focus on formative assessment or the integration of social and emotional competencies were implemented and data showed the positive impact on student learning, these were added to the beliefs and values. The mission statement became a living document, ever changing based on new learning about what worked. Through PLC conversations, educators became the decision-makers on what beliefs and values supported the mission.

The mission now reflected the collective commitment to these practices, and it clearly demonstrated how collegiality and collaboration moved the school closer to achieving its goals. The actions the school staff engaged in through the CAR process were led by a principal who understood the importance of reculturing the school. As Fullan notes, "Reculturing is the name of the game. Much change is structural and superficial. Transforming culture—changing what people in the organization value and how they work together to accomplish it—leads to deep, lasting change" (Fullan, 2002, p. 17).

## SHARED LEADERSHIP

> There is evidence to suggest that student outcomes are more likely to improve where leadership sources are distributed throughout the school and where teachers are empowered in decisions related to teaching, learning, and assessment (Silins and Mulford, 2002).

The intent of the PLC process within CAR is to return ownership and decision-making for curriculum, instruction, and assessment to educators. The CAR process is the very definition of shared instructional leadership. In the CAR process, everyone, including those in formal leadership roles, is a learner.

A 2010 Wallace Study on the links between leadership and student learning found that when principals and teachers share leadership, teachers' working relationships are stronger and student achievement is higher (Seashore-Louis, Leithwood, Walstrom, and Anderson, 2010). When teachers collectively take responsibility for student learning, teacher leadership flourishes.

As formal leaders provide educators with the time, the focus and the ability to make decisions about their professional practice in a collegial environment, they build collective efficacy and shared accountability. When the principal communicates that every teacher is a leader if they bring ideas and resources to the PLC table in order to improve student learning outcomes, a culture of shared leadership begins to take hold.

Shared leadership can, of course, take other forms, such as teacher participation in formal committees and other school and district decision-making bodies. However, simply being named to these committees is not enough. The work must be collaborative, authentic, and lead to agreements that are based on consensus on the actions that will support the shared mission. In the next chapter, you will see how another key collaborative structure can greatly impact not only student learning but the climate in which that learning exists.

## COHERENCE

Picture a car on the road trying to avoid a number of barriers, detours, and side trips that make traveling to the destination a difficult journey. Schools that are focused on compliance and programs instead of process and practices are generally not engaged in reflecting on the impact this is having on both school climate and student learning. They are often moving in several different directions creating a feeling of disjointedness and a "this too shall pass," mentality. They fail to engage in deeper dialogue that results in a shared understanding of how their leader and educator practices make the difference when it comes to achieving their collective mission.

Creating coherence, the purpose of the CAR framework, is achieved by maintaining a focus on key elements of effective schools. Over time, as principals and teachers work together to achieve a common mission, they build a deep understanding of how their actions support learning for every student. External forces such as state mandates can now be viewed through the lens of how they impact the work of the school. Collaborative decisions can be made on how to best address the mandates while keeping focused on the destination.

## TRUST

Trust is only developed through consistent actions on the part of the school leader and educators who support the shared commitment to achieving a common mission. The actions of each adult determine the level of trust experienced by all. Consequently, trust is the result of:

- Collaborating to develop a shared mission supported by agreed-upon values and beliefs
- Providing the time, tools, and structure for authentic collaborative professional learning focused on student learning
- Consistently adhering to and holding one another accountable for agreed-upon expectations and norms that support professional collaboration
- Consistently modeling the behaviors expected to be emulated by students
- Engaging in shared leadership practices that support shared ownership and shared responsibility for student success
- A willingness to confront issues and barriers to achieving the shared mission

You may want to utilize the tool, Professional Climate: What is Our Current Reality?, found in Appendix K to allow the professional staff to assess the current status of the components of a collegial climate. This can inform the actions the school will take to build a strong collaborative culture.

## CLOSING

This chapter focused on creating a collegial climate for educators so they can effectively collaborate to support the success of all students. The climate for educators and students is tightly connected. Chapter 4 introduces a schoolwide PLC, the School Climate Team. Just as the PLC teams in chapter 3 use 10 conversations to drive the learning cycle, the School Climate Team tackles 10 conversations that will help ensure a cycle of school climate improvement for both students and adults.

*CAUTION:* Although chapters 2–4 deal with different components of CAR, it is imperative to remember that the pieces of the framework are interconnected. CAR represents a systemic process, not a linear one. Schools must engage both curriculum-related PLCs and School Climate Teams by providing them with the tools and conversations to improve both the learning cycle and the cycle of continuous school climate improvement. Both types of collaborative teams simultaneously impact the journey toward higher levels of student learning.

## REFERENCES

Fullan, M. (2002, May). The change leader. *Educational Leadership* 17(59), 8.

Hargreaves, A., and Fullan, M. (2012). *Professional capital: Transforming teaching in every school.* New York: Teachers College Press.

Hattie, J. (2009). *Visible learning: A synthesis of over 800 meta-analyses relating to achievement.* New York: Routledge.

Seashore-Louis, K., Leithwood, K., Walstrom, K.L., and Anderson, S. E. (2010). *Learning from leadership: Investigating the links to improved student learning.* University of Minnesota Center for Applied Research and Educational Improvement.

Shah, M. (2012). The importance and benefits of teacher collegiality in schools a literature review. *Procedia - Social and Behavioral Sciences* 46, 1242–1246.

Silins, H., and Mulford, B. (2002). Schools as learning organizations: The case for system, teacher and student learning. *Educational Administration* 40, 425–446.

# Chapter 4

# Ensuring a Smooth Journey

## *Collaboratively Improving School Climate*

> Empowering our teams through meaningful conversations that lead to positive change is my leadership goal. The CAR framework has provided the leverage we needed to move forward as a school community, building a collaborative environment in which shared leadership drives our decisions. This shared effort has fostered a positive school climate that has productively engaged students and successfully reduced chronic absenteeism.—Jennifer Marinello, Principal, Hamilton Township Public Schools

The CAR framework identifies three key components of school culture: the climate for learning, shared leadership and the communication of connections and high expectations. Climate is often described as how people feel in a school, while the culture is dependent on the actions of those in the school. Culture is often best described as "the way we do things around here." Feelings and actions are tightly connected. The CAR engages educators to embrace new ways of thinking that require changing "the way we do things." These actions result in changes in the way both educators and students feel about being in school. As a school embraces CAR, the climate will change and as they stay on the course the culture of CAR will take hold.

As noted in chapter 3, a collaborative culture marked by collective reflection on student learning, shared leadership and coherence results in a positive climate for adult learning. This chapter will focus on the climate for learning for students.

The climate for students and the climate for educators are interdependent. A positive school climate for students and adults that is focused on the growth of every student is the foundation for effective teaching and learning. There is a compelling body of research that underscores this reality. Positive school climates promote academic achievement, healthy social and emotional development and increased teacher retention.

**Roadblock Thinking: School climate will fix itself.**

Although educators know the importance of a safe and supportive learning environment, school climate improvement is often not tackled in a comprehensive

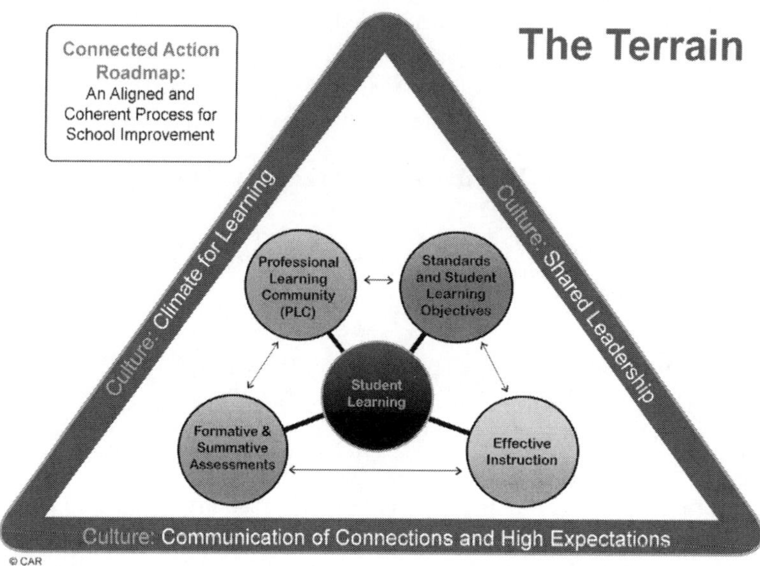


**Figure 4.1 CAR Model: Culture.**

and targeted fashion. It is one of those areas that gets the short shrift or is addressed through the implementation of a variety of programs. Problems that arise related to school climate issues are often addressed using a Band-Aid approach.

**Forward Thinking: School climate improvement requires a deliberate plan.**

A collaboratively developed school climate improvement plan based on school climate data is an essential tool in implementing a deliberate and targeted approach to enhancing the school climate. Just as the PLC team described in chapter 2 is integral to a continuous improvement of curriculum, instruction and assessment, there needs to be a PLC team dedicated to a continuous cycle of school climate improvement.

## THE SCHOOL CLIMATE TEAM

A School Climate Team should be established to lead school climate improvement efforts. The purpose of this professional learning team is to focus on exploring best practices in school climate improvement, collecting data, setting goals and implementing a plan of action that will support the highest levels of learning, both academic and social and emotional.

A school's climate is the responsibility of everyone who is part of that school community. The team must model shared leadership and shared responsibility by ensuring a broad representation of stakeholders.

Consider the following questions when forming the School Climate Team:

1. Does the team include representation from teachers across the grade levels?

2. What other staff roles should be included: nurses, support services personnel, paraprofessionals, school resource officers?
3. How will students be engaged in the work of the team? Students' voice is essential to climate improvement. School climate improvement is not something that is done to students, it is only accomplished if everyone in the school community takes responsibility and shares leadership in making it happen—that certainly includes the students.
4. Does the team include representation from those involved in after-school or extra-curricular activities? School climate does not end when school is dismissed. It is an integral part of sports teams, clubs, and other school-sponsored activities.
5. Does the principal play an active role? Principals should not direct the team, but instead, foster meaningful collaboration. School leaders must be engaged team members and send a strong message that school climate work is essential and valued.

## THE WORK OF THE SCHOOL CLIMATE TEAM

Like the grade-level and content area PLCs, the CAR provides 10 Conversations to guide the work of the School Climate Team. The 10 CAR School Climate Team Conversations guide the team in setting up a process of continuous climate improvement. The goal of this chapter is to understand why each conversation is important and what questions School Climate Teams need to grapple with, not to prescribe the answers. The answers will come from the collaborative work of the team who understands their current context and can seek targeted information for the answers that will best serve their school. Remember, CAR recognizes the ineffectiveness of simply prescribing a program. Instead, we focus on the process schools must use to create a tailored plan to meet the needs of their school community.

CAR recognizes that educators have many tools—their own knowledge and expertise, plentiful research and numerous professional resources and programs that highlight best practices. What teams may not have is a continuous process that uses these tools to collaboratively develop their approach to improving school climate. The 10 School Climate Team Conversations can be found in Appendix L.

### Conversation 1: Create a Common Language. What Is School Climate?

Before beginning any work, School Climate Team members must reach a common understanding of what school climate is. Establishing a common definition to guide the work is the focus of the first conversation. The National School Climate Centre has developed a comprehensive definition of school climate (see Appendix M) that could serve this purpose.

Each dimension of school climate is defined by a list of major indicators. The list of indicators is not exhaustive, and a team may want to modify this definition to include other indicators that are especially important in their school environment. In a large school district, agreeing on the same climate definition creates a common focus and allows School Climate Teams from across the district to share best practices.

## Conversation 2: Examine the Climate for Adults

Although relationships are only one component of school climate, they are the most important. Educators often focus on the relationships between students; however, it is essential for the School Climate Team to consider four sets of relationships:

- Student to Student
- Adult to Student
- Student to Adult
- Adult to Adult

Although adult relationships certainly include relationships with parents and community members, this conversation focuses on the collaboration of the professional staff. The professional staff must be models for the type of adult relationships expected at every level. The School Climate Team should lead the examination of the components of a collegial climate described in chapter 3, using data to examine each and creating plans to address existing barriers to effective collaboration.

## Conversation 3: Assess the Current Reality

This conversation begins with a simple question. What initiatives or programs are currently in place to address the various dimensions of school climate? Teams should make a list of initiatives, programs, and activities that are being implemented throughout the school in order to support a positive learning environment.

**Roadblock Thinking: A positive school climate can be established by implementing a variety of programs and activities.**

This way of thinking is supported by the number of programs available through vendors and professional learning consultants that focus on aspects of school climate, such as anti-bullying, conflict resolution, social and emotional learning, trauma-informed instruction, restorative justice, and so on. Couple this with the addition of activities, such as assembly presentations, "student of the month" awards, community service projects, and so on, and the result can be a chaotic implementation of disjointed programs, activities, and initiatives that leave staff feeling confused and overwhelmed. If the staff does not understand the purpose of each program, then what are the chances the students are making those connections? How will educators know if the initiatives are achieving their intended goals?

**Forward Thinking: Schools need to implement a targeted and coherent school climate improvement plan.**

Programs and initiatives will not change the school climate. Each of the previously mentioned examples of programs and activities may be quite worthwhile, but not without a plan that focuses on the systemic processes and practices that impact implementation. In order to ensure coherence and avoid initiative fatigue, the team should examine each program that is currently in place using a set of guiding questions. These questions also need to be answered before implementing any new initiatives.

- What is the goal of the program, activity, or initiative? What need is it addressing?
- Is it achieving that goal and effectively addressing the need? What data supports this answer? Consider conducting student focus groups to determine if students value the program, activity, or initiative.
- Should the school keep, modify, or abandon this program?
- If the program or initiative remains or needs to be modified is there a clear purpose and goal for doing so? How will the team communicate this program's connection to the overall school climate improvement plan? How will the team know if the program or initiative is successful?

## Conversation 4: Social and Emotional Learning (SEL)

Educators have long recognized the importance of attending to the needs of the whole child, however, focusing on the social and emotional needs of the student through additional lessons and programs is sometimes viewed as just one more thing on teachers' plates.

**Roadblock Thinking: Emphasis on academic achievement and assessment results means that teaching content knowledge and skills should take precedence over instruction in SEL.**

In the so-called era of school reform, emphasis was placed on ensuring equity by focusing on the statewide assessment of students in relation to standards. State assessment results became a fixation as they were published as the sole barometer of a school district's success. Assessment results also drove determinations of individual teacher effectiveness. The pressure to achieve on "the test" took the emphasis away from the importance of educating the whole child.

**Forward Thinking: SEL results in higher levels of student achievement. Social and emotional learning instruction provides a foundation for a safe and positive learning environment, and enhances students' ability to succeed in school, career, and life.**

Since the pandemic, the phrase, "Maslow before Bloom" is often heard as a rebuke of roadblock thinking. School communities have become acutely aware of the need to prioritize children's social and emotional well-being. The Collaborative for Academic and Social Emotional Learning (CASEL) has developed the framework in figure 4.2 that identifies five key SEL competencies.

There is a deep connection between SEL and school climate. Consider the following quote:

> Key aspects of school climate—conditions for learning (e.g., physical and emotional safety, connectedness and support, engaging and challenging opportunities to learn,

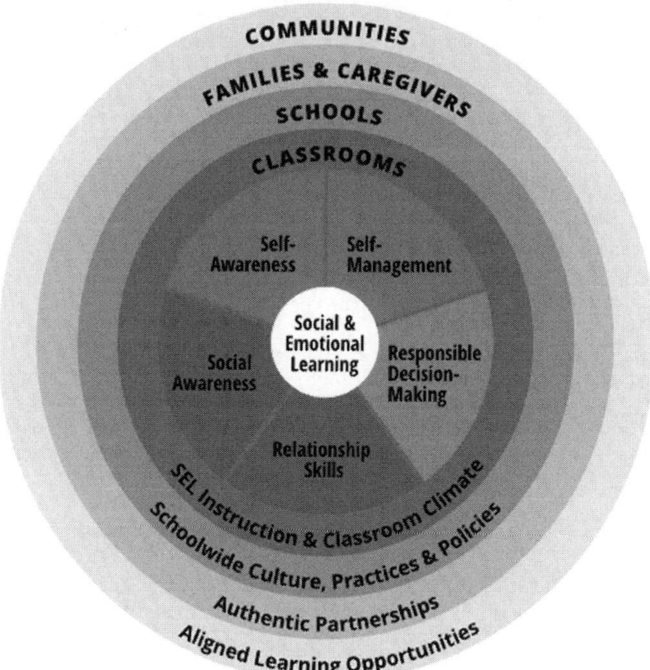


**Figure 4.2 CASEL SEL Framework.** https://casel.org/fundamentals-of-sel/what-is-the-casel-framework/#interactive-casel-wheel; ©2020 CASEL. Social and Emotional Learning Framework. All rights reserved. casel.org.

> and interactions with and modeling from socially and emotionally competent adults and peers)—and SEL are interconnected. SEL cannot flourish in a school independent of positive and supportive school and classroom climates, just as systematic efforts to build student and adult social and emotional competencies contribute to nurturing classroom and school climates. (Berg, Osher, Moroney, and Yoder, 2017. p. 4)

SEL is best envisioned through the lens of a tiered system of support that strategically embeds SEL across the school—in classrooms, home, and community.

Tier One, as shown in figure 4.3, provides the focus for Conversation 4.

Relationships are a key component of school climate. In Conversation 4, the School Climate Team must consider what SEL skills should be taught to every student in order to build positive relationships at all levels. Consider the impact that conflict has on relationships in the school environment. Teachers and administrators spend a significant amount of time intervening in conflict situations. Conflict can result in negative feelings that certainly impact a students' sense of safety and their ability to focus on their learning. Explicit teaching of social and emotional learning skills related to conflict can effectively serve as a springboard for building a Tier One approach to SEL.

Below is a set of lessons that one school adopted schoolwide. The lessons' objectives were developed by the School Climate Team to define skills, knowledge, and

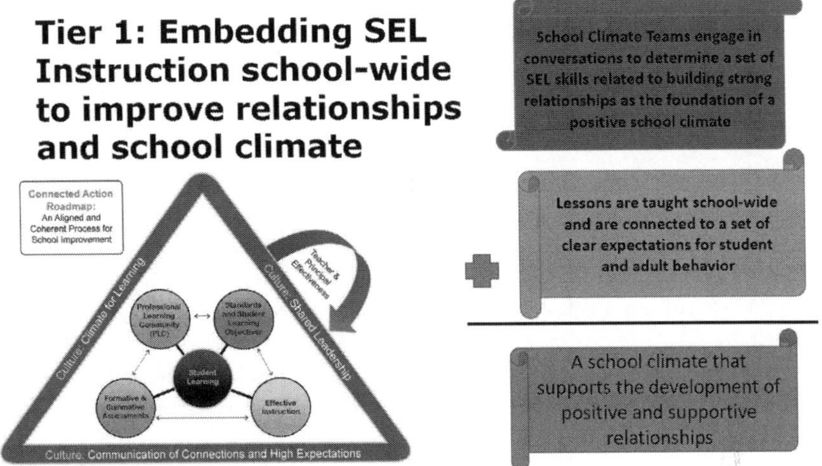


**Figure 4.3 Tier 1 SEL.**

understandings that students need in order to deal with conflict—both bullying and normal conflict.

- Understand the difference between bullying and normal conflict
- Identify aggressive, passive, and assertive behavior
- Use appropriate "I" Messages
- Identify the difference between telling and tattling (reporting and ratting)
- Demonstrate good bystander (upstander) behavior
- Resolve normal conflicts peacefully

The purpose of these lessons was to improve relationships, provide a common language related to conflict, set clear expectations for how students deal with conflict and reduce the number of conflicts experienced at school.

*Considerations for Building Effective Schoolwide SEL Instruction*

- Schoolwide SEL lessons are taught by everyone in the school. If only the school counselor teaches the lessons, they will not have an impact on the overall climate of the building.
- The School Climate Team should consider choosing a limited number of lessons. The goal is to select a set of lessons that can be taught and consistently reinforced. No teacher has the time to teach a large number of required schoolwide lessons. Tier 2 will allow teachers to address additional SEL competencies through content area instruction.
- The same lesson objectives should be taught using developmentally appropriate activities at each grade level. This creates consistent messaging and the opportunity for students to continue to hone these skills as they move from grade level to grade level. New lessons can be added at any point to address a particular need the team has identified.

- All staff members (teachers, paraprofessionals, office/cafeteria/custodial staff, bus drivers) are trained. Skills are taught and modeled consistently by all staff. This creates a common language about conflict and over time the expectation for everyone to apply these skills becomes embedded in the school culture.
- SEL skills are connected to the student code of conduct and discussions related to discipline.
- Skills are reinforced on a schoolwide and classroom level throughout the school year.
- Parents are trained so that they can reinforce the skills at home. Students should understand that these are lifelong skills that should be applied in situations outside of school.
- Instruction is integrated into the curriculum across grade levels and content areas. Every teacher should take the opportunity to reinforce schoolwide lessons by making connections to their classroom expectations as well as the content they teach.
- Social and emotional skill development should be assessed to determine the impact of instruction. What is the evidence that students are able to apply these skills?

In Tier 2, shown in figure 4.4, PLCs are charged with creating student-friendly learning objectives linked to the SEL competencies. These SEL skills are taught to enhance the learning of the academic content. This produces a curriculum that equitably addresses both academic and social-emotional learning. Students are immersed in experiences that help them in developing specific SEL skills, and in applying them in order to achieve their academic goals.

In Tier 3, students who struggle with social and emotional competencies are provided more intensive support by school counselors, social workers, or school psychologists. These students may also be referred to professionals outside of the school.

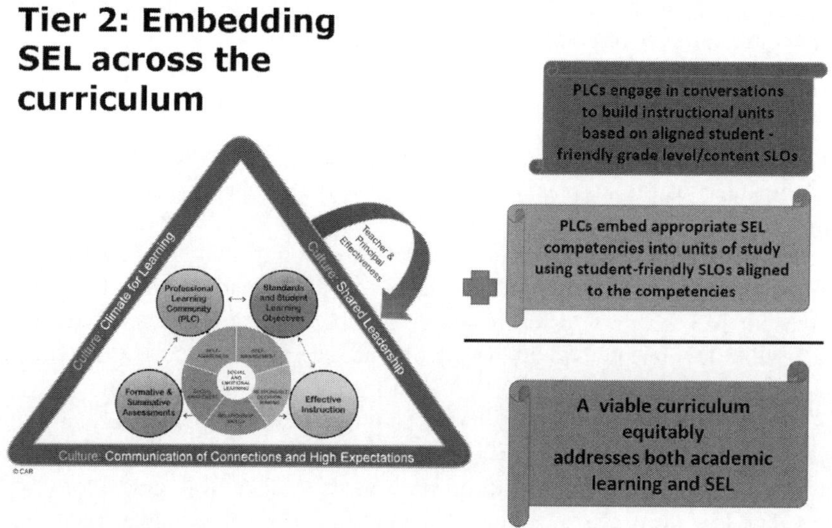


**Figure 4.4 Tier 2 SEL.**

When the School Climate Team engages in Conversation 4, it is focused on schoolwide implementation. However, in order for students to engage meaningfully in the development of social and emotional well-being, it is important for the School Climate Team to advocate for the development of a three-tiered comprehensive approach.

## Conversation 5: Identify Sources of School Climate Assessment Data

Data, both formal and informal, quantitative, and qualitative, are an essential tool in ensuring that the School Climate Team creates a continuous cycle of school climate improvement. Schools have a wealth of data that the team could consider such as disciplinary referrals, bullying reports, suspension and expulsion data, academic grade distributions, attendance records for students and staff, parental concerns, teacher turnover, and student graduation rates.

The team should strongly consider administering a school climate survey. Such comprehensive surveys can provide an assessment of several components of school climate. The surveys are usually completed by students, parents, and staff, providing valuable data based on each group's perspective. Once school climate surveys are administered and analyzed, the School Climate Team can identify targeted sources of other data that will provide additional insight.

Focus groups can also prove to be a valuable tool for digging more deeply into areas of concern. Teams should be mindful of diversity and equity when selecting focus group participants. Serious consideration must be given to who participates, what questions are asked, how they are asked and how the data are recorded.

Finally, the School Climate Rubric can help the team and the school staff to not only understand the key components of school climate improvement but to define the ultimate desired outcome. Please note that the complete CAR Rubric, Appendix M, will be discussed in chapter 5. The School Climate Team should focus on the indicators of the CAR Rubric that are related to the element of culture. The culture element of the CAR Rubric contains 15 indicators related to school climate and culture and features four performance levels. The performance levels are not intended to be evaluative; rather their descriptions support understanding the actions that serve to advance a positive school climate. School climate improvement is a journey. Moving from one performance level to another takes time. The School Climate Rubric is an essential tool that will assist the team along the way. This rubric is a subset of the full CAR Rubric that will be addressed in chapter 5.

## Conversation 6: Analyze School Climate Data

Analyzing school climate data involves using the information to identify specific ways that the strengths of the current school climate can be maintained, while enhancing the weaker areas. The following questions can guide the team in its analysis:

1. What strength(s) can be identified from this data?
2. What factors seem to be contributing to making this a strength?
3. What need(s) can be identified from this data?
4. What factors seem to be contributing to creating this need?

5. What is the priority of the needs identified?
6. What existing programs/initiatives are currently intended to address the needs? Do they need to be kept, modified, or abandoned?
7. What other strategies could be used for addressing each of these needs? What current strengths can be leveraged to address these needs?
8. What are the roadblocks that could derail the solution or strategy? How can we address the potential roadblocks?
9. Who needs to be involved in planning and implementation?
10. What does success look like?

There is one more piece of important data that the team should consider before moving to Conversation 7. After reviewing the 10 School Climate Team Conversations that are presented in this chapter, the team may want to consider setting process goals as well as outcome goals. What conversations has the team had? What conversations does the team need to have before developing the plan? For example, has the team agreed on a common definition of school climate? Has it done an inventory of current programs and initiatives? These conversations take time and are part of the school climate improvement process.

### Conversation 7: Develop the School Climate Improvement Plan

Once the team has identified priority goals, it is time to develop a concrete plan of action that provides direction, organization, and a timeline. The components of an action plan include:

- A well-defined description of the goal to be achieved
- Action steps that need to be carried out to reach the goal
- Assignment of people in charge of carrying out each step
- A timeline of when steps will be completed
- Resources needed to complete steps
- Formative and summative measures of progress

The steps to creating a viable school climate improvement plan include:

- Develop the goal(s). Does it meet the SMART criteria? Is it **s**pecific, **m**easurable, **a**ttainable, **r**elevant, and **t**imely?
- List the actions that will be taken to achieve the goal(s).
- Who is responsible for each action?
- Develop realistic deadlines for each action step.
- Determine the evidence of success?
- Establish both formative and summative assessments.
- Identify the resources needed. Consider time, use of facilities, technology support, communication tools, materials, and expenses.
- Allocate time to analyze formative data throughout the process in order to adjust the plan as needed.
- Don't forget to celebrate and communicate successes along the way. This builds momentum and supports sustainability.

## Conversation 8: Focus on Communication and Community Engagement

Ownership of the school climate is everyone's responsibility: students, staff, parents, and the community. The school climate improvement plan will only be successful if everyone understands the purpose of the plan, what needs it is targeting, what outcomes the School Climate Team is hoping to achieve and how those outcomes will positively impact students. The School Climate Team must begin by sharing what was learned through the needs assessment process. Next, the team must clearly illustrate how the school climate improvement plan will address the identified needs while sustaining the current strengths. The team should identify the role students, staff, parents and community members have in making the plan a success. The team must consider how it will consistently update stakeholders throughout the year on progress toward achieving the plan goals, making sure to celebrate successes and to ask for additional support when facing potential barriers.

Students' voice is extremely important. Students should be involved in each step of the plan development and implementation process. Having student ambassadors communicate the importance of the plan to other students and community members can be a powerful way to message shared ownership and shared responsibility for school climate improvement.

Explore the potential communication tools that could be used to update everyone frequently and consistently. The team can consider school and community events, as well as utilize multiple social media outlets. When members of the school community are aware of school climate improvement efforts and celebrate successes along the way, they begin to develop shared values and beliefs about the type of learning environment that is important for all students. As this process continues each year, these shared beliefs and values begin to shift the deeper school culture, strengthening the sustainability of school climate improvement efforts.

## Conversation 9: Implement the Plan and Use Formative Data/Benchmarks to Make Adjustments

During implementation, the School Climate Team meets to reflect on how the school climate improvement plan and strategies are working. By reviewing and analyzing formative data throughout the year, the team can identify needed adjustments and respond to obstacles as they arise. The team should include formative feedback from other stakeholders during this reflective process to gain different perspectives about how the process of implementation is going. Teams can also identify opportunities to celebrate successes.

## Conversation 10: Analyze Summative Data and Reflect and Revise School Climate Plan

At the end of the year, the team reviews the summative assessment data and considers the following:

- What progress was made toward achieving each goal?
- What barriers remain to achieving each goal?

- What goals should be carried over to the next school climate improvement plan?
- Again, it is important to secure summative feedback from different stakeholder groups. How do they view the progress made during the year? What might have made the plan more successful?
- Reassess the Culture element using the CAR Rubric. What actions will be required to move to the next level of performance?

Conversation 10 provides new information that will deepen the discussions as the team revisits the 10 CAR School Climate Team Conversations and the cycle of school climate improvement begins again.

## DON'T FORGET TO CELEBRATE

Schoolwide celebrations are a chance to bring together students, staff, parents and community members. Celebrating along the journey of continuous school climate improvement presents a unique opportunity to develop a sense of community built on shared goals, shared values and shared beliefs. When celebrations are built around a clear message that articulates what the school values, all stakeholders begin to internalize those values.

Planning impactful celebrations is part of the role of the School Climate team. The team should consider the following questions when planning a celebration:

- What is the clear message the team wants to send to the school community? How does the message relate to a school value the team wants the community to embrace? What impact does the team hope the celebration has on students? On staff? On parents/community members?
- What type of celebration would best communicate the message? Be sure to include students in the planning and implementation of celebrations.
- How does the message support school climate improvement efforts?
- How will the message continue to be reinforced once the celebration has occurred? For example, having a celebration related to valuing diversity will not be impactful unless the team plans other ways to consistently reinforce that message over time.

Yearly school themes help to establish an overall message for the school year. They help to unify everyone in the school community around a common idea. Themes can be woven through schoolwide events, as well as, across content area curriculum. The greater school community should also be encouraged to take part in messaging the school theme, from the PTA/PTO to local businesses. Yearly themes can become a tradition with students playing an active role in choosing or creating the theme.

The School Climate Team in one school decided to set a goal to engage more students to be upstanders instead of bystanders in bullying incidents. All the students were taught upstander strategies as part of Tier One SEL instruction. In order to unify the school around this effort, the students choose the theme, "Be a Hero!" Students of the Month, usually acknowledged for academic success, became Heroes of the Month for applying the schoolwide SEL skills focused on fostering positive relationships.

The local pizza shop provided gift certificates to these heroes so they could celebrate their accomplishments with their families. Schoolwide celebrations, such as Veteran's Day, focused on heroes in the community. Teachers embedded the theme in their content by focusing on heroes in literature, history, science, and math.

## CLOSING

The 10 conversations, along with the planning of meaningful celebrations, will support the School Climate Team as they develop, foster, maintain and continuously improve the school climate.

The CAR framework outlined thus far focuses on collaboration as the key to improving teaching and learning in a culture that supports a continuous school improvement cycle. Shared leadership for CAR starts with the initial planning for implementation. Chapter 5 will highlight key tools, strategies and factors that need to be considered as your school begins the CAR journey.

## REFERENCES

Berg, J., Osher, D., Moroney, D., and Yoder, N. (February 2017). *The intersection of school climate and social and emotional development.* Washington, DC: American Institutes for Research.

# *Chapter 5*

# Leading the CAR Journey toward the Ultimate Destination

> Although I recognized the importance of teacher leadership, school culture and shared values, I believed that these were often perceived as nebulous and abstract in nature. The day-to-day work of CAR—standards-based instructional units, high-quality assessments, data-driven conversations and instructional decision-making—translated these abstract components into real-world tools for teachers. By using these as a vehicle, modeling and encouraging teacher leadership and changes in the culture, the positive momentum occurred organically. That in turn, has given us a much better chance of having this school improvement process institutionalized.
>
> —Anthony Petruzzelli, Superintendent, Westampton Public School District

## PREPARING FOR THE JOURNEY

On a daily basis, school and district leaders are faced with multiple challenges and decisions about the best investment of their time in order to strengthen student learning, build teacher capacity, and ensure equitable access to high-quality curriculum and instruction for each student. The CAR framework offers a systems-based approach to address these priorities, but the question remains—How is this system created? It is created collaboratively! Leaders need to consider how CAR supports the current vision and mission of the school or district and then assemble a leadership team that is representative of all roles, including teacher leaders, to craft a vision for CAR and to guide its implementation. Collaboration and shared leadership are hallmarks of the CAR framework and therefore, they must be evident throughout all stages of CAR implementation. The CAR framework offers a range of powerful tools and strategies to support the CAR Leadership Team in their work. The CAR Planning Guide, found in Appendix N, summarizes much of the content of this chapter into a tool that leadership teams may find helpful.

## ARE WE READY?

The first step taken by leaders who effectively implement CAR is to consider the "readiness" level of their school or district. Components of readiness include organizational structures, a shared vision for the work, and an honest appraisal of where the school/district is in relation to the elements of the CAR.

Specific organizational structures need to be in place before CAR can be implemented with fidelity. Perhaps, the most critical structure is consistent and dedicated time for collaborative learning teams to meet on a regular basis to engage in the CAR conversations. Ideally, this takes place weekly and does not compete with the daily prep period of teachers. While the CAR conversations ensure a targeted focus on curriculum, instruction, and assessment, only through the commitment of the leader and the team members can this time be protected from other competing tasks and priorities. It's all too easy for a principal to ask the team to address grade-level housekeeping items such as the planning of a field trip or assembly presentation during PLC time. When the principal or supervisor refrains from doing this, a clear message is sent about the critical importance of the CAR conversations and the collaborative, instructional work taking place during PLC time.

The CAR framework is built on a vision of curriculum as a process rather than a product and through that process, PLC teams create the curriculum one conversation at a time over the course of a multi-year period. This represents a significant departure from traditional approaches to curriculum writing. Consequently, leaders need to address how this new process will integrate with current organizational structures and roles dedicated to curriculum development. For example, if curriculum teams typically convene during the summer to write/update curricula, how will that work be integrated with CAR? Many districts have shifted this work to the grade-level PLC teams who determine which conversations will be their focus. Once the standards have been unpacked and the learning goals have been placed in the template, planning for instruction can begin and decisions will need to be made about which conversations will be tackled and when, creating a timeline for instructional unit development. Content supervisors, who traditionally oversaw summer curriculum writing projects, play a powerful role in coaching these teams, ensuring vertical articulation, and offering support in a wide variety of ways including resource selection and assessment decisions.

In earlier chapters, roadblock thinking and forward thinking were discussed (Appendix A). From the leader's perspective, these undoubtedly provide an initial glimpse into readiness levels in terms of mindset. It is essential to remember that CAR will require educators to shift perspective and challenge roadblock thinking that is the result of "the way things have always been done." As leadership seeks to redefine the work of PLCs and revamp the definition of curriculum, educators will need time to process these shifts and to embrace forward thinking. It is important for the leadership team to utilize consistent messaging related to roadblock and forward thinking. Leadership cannot wait to build collaborative structures until they achieve total "buy-in." As educators work in collaborative teams and students reap the rewards of their efforts, they will experience and internalize the benefits of forward thinking.

The concrete organizational structures identified above are essential components of CAR "readiness." Integral to the work of the leadership team is their ability to articulate a clear vision of CAR as a collaborative process. The vision should be grounded in the district's or school's "why." Questions that the leadership team should consider include:

- Why do we want to implement CAR?
- What are our desired outcomes?
- How will it guide the work of all educators?
- How will it shift our current processes?
- How will it foster shared leadership? Teacher leadership?
- How will it impact teaching and learning?
- How will it enhance the climate for learning for both students and adults?

The answers to these questions need to be broadly and consistently shared with all stakeholders.

In addition to organizational structures and vision building, leaders need to know where they are on the roadmap. One very powerful tool that can clearly articulate starting points and readiness is the CAR Rubric found in Appendix O. With a focus on growth, the rubric provides an opportunity for all educators involved in CAR implementation to authentically assess the current context. This aggregated data provides the leadership team with a shared understanding of the current context and supports rich conversations around starting points that promote student growth.

Organizational structures, vision building, and an honest appraisal of starting points provide leaders with a baseline for CAR readiness. These components are the foundational pieces necessary in order to create a realistic and actionable implementation plan. In the authors' work with schools implementing CAR, teachers often voice their recognition of the value of the processes embedded in the framework. Educators want to step out of their silos, collaborate with their colleagues and they recognize that sharing the workload and learning from each other will not only be rewarding, but will maximize student learning. However, they just as readily share their fears that there will be no follow-through, that they won't be provided the time to work collaboratively or that they will begin the CAR process only to have another new initiative take its place before it has time to take hold and make a difference. The leadership team must demonstrate their commitment to CAR, by leveraging educators' passion and excitement about the potential benefits and by taking actions to prevent the fears from becoming realities. Now, let's explore the tools that will support the CAR Leadership Team in implementing the process.

## THE CAR LEADERSHIP TOOLKIT

### Supporting Tool: The CAR Implementation Planning Guide

One recurring theme throughout the earlier chapters of this book is the understanding that CAR is a process—not a program, initiative, or mandate. This essential feature allows schools and districts to implement CAR in a way that makes sense for their unique context while at the same time remaining faithful to the core tenets of the framework. The CAR Planning Guide (Appendix N) provides leadership teams with a tool to support decision-making as they engage in the planning process. It addresses key areas such as vision building, identifying essential structures, developing a multi-year implementation plan, communicating with stakeholders, providing professional learning and coaching support, and integrating steps to ensure sustainability and coherence. The guide is not intended to be prescriptive or linear. It is offered in the spirit of collaboration, addressing the vital elements necessary to implement a continuous cycle of improvement through the CAR framework while at the same time providing for adaptation at the local level. Central to the success of the Connected Action Roadmap is effective leadership and a shared vision of what that looks like in practice.

## Supporting Tool: The CAR Rubric

The CAR Rubric (Appendix O) is comprised of five elements—(1) Standards, Student Learning Objectives, and Effective Instruction; (2) Assessment; (3) Professional Learning Communities; (4) Culture; and (5) Teacher and Principal Effectiveness. It is designed as an instrument for growth, not evaluation, and the quality levels—Not Addressed, Emerging, Developing, and Sustaining—support this mindset. The data derived from the rubric assessments by all educators involved in CAR support teams in identifying current and future priorities as well as measuring growth from year to year. All too often, educators and teams neglect to celebrate the small wins and the growth exemplified through consistent use of the rubric serves to both motivate and refocus the teams when necessary.

It is essential that leaders regularly devote time to their own professional learning needs. Utilizing the CAR Rubric, which is aligned to the Professional Standards for School Leaders (PSEL), promotes greater coherence between leadership practices, annual goals and the professional learning opportunities in which leaders engage. From a leadership team perspective, this rubric also promotes rich conversations that build bridges between actionable steps, professional learning, and the systems-based CAR framework that leaders are implementing to strengthen teacher practice and student learning. The New Jersey Principals and Supervisors Association (NJPSA) has created an online tool that leaders at every level can utilize to reflect on the actions they are taking to support the PSEL. Modeling the collaborative process of CAR, a group of district and school leaders unpacked the PSEL into clear specific actions that leaders need to take in order to operationalize the standards. The NJPSA PSEL Reflection and Growth Tool also includes information on how district and school leadership teams might utilize the PSEL to collaboratively engage in dialogue about how the standards are driving district and school improvement efforts. This tool can be accessed at https://njpsa.org/psel-leadership-reflection-and-growth-tool/.

## Supporting Tool: The PLC Conversations

At the heart of the CAR framework, is the series of focused conversations to guide the work of PLCs, including both the grade-level/content area PLC and the School

Climate Team, as delineated in chapter 2 and chapter 4, respectively. The 10 PLC Conversations (Appendix B) ensure a consistent focus on curriculum, instruction, and assessment and are grounded in an iterative process through which the teams collaboratively solve problems emerging throughout the teaching-learning cycle. Once the CAR Leadership Team decides the grade levels and content areas that will engage in the initial phase of the CAR implementation, educators can begin the work of instructional unit design using the 10 PLC Conversations.

The PLC process engages educators in solving problems that are directly related to the learning goals of the students with whom they are currently working. This is the power of CAR—the collaborative, problem-solving nature and laser focus on student learning of the teams. Through this work, teacher leadership emerges organically. Schools and districts that have implemented CAR with fidelity have found that the teams work and lead independently.

No longer do principals or other building administrators need to be present as ownership for curriculum, instruction, and assessment is assumed by the team. The grade-level/content PLCs share leadership often through a rotating role or other collaborative measures. As this transfer of responsibility occurs from administrator to PLC, the administrator is able to work with the teams on a different level. Guiding questions for leaders as they periodically engage in the PLC meetings are also provided in this tool. Additionally, many administrators dive more deeply into areas of need with the teams based on the data emerging throughout the process. This type of job-embedded professional learning for all involved is invaluable and strengthens instructional leadership at each level.

The School Climate Team utilizes the 10 School Climate Team Conversations (Appendix L) examined in chapter 4 to guide the team in establishing a process of continuous school climate improvement by engaging all stakeholders in the process. Just as the grade-level/content area PLCs share leadership for teaching and learning, the School Climate Team creates the opportunity for shared leadership and collective ownership of a positive climate that is conducive to the learning for both students and adults.

### Supporting Tool: Standards for Professional Learning and CAR

As leaders strategically plan professional development opportunities, it is important to note that CAR aligns with the Standards for Professional Learning. The Crosswalk between the Standards for Professional Learning and CAR can be found in Appendix P. We know that deep professional learning that takes place within the PLCs builds the collective capacity of educators to address curriculum, instruction, and assessment. However, there may also be a need to provide additional, targeted professional learning. Leaders must consider the purpose of these opportunities as well as how the professional learning will be applied through the PLC conversations.

### Supporting Tool: The Leadership Roles within CAR

While a shared vision for CAR is essential, understanding what this looks like at each of the leadership levels within the central office and the school buildings is equally important. The tool, Leadership Roles within CAR (Appendix Q), articulates both common responsibilities across the roles as well as those unique to each position. For example, establishing and facilitating a vision for a systemic approach to continuous district improvement focused on student learning clearly begins at the top with the superintendent. However, all of the leadership roles have ownership of this through specific action steps unique to their role. Leadership teams need to engage in dialogue around these responsibilities and shift from Roadblock Thinking to Forward Thinking (Appendix A). Not only does this foster a more effective implementation of CAR, it supports the sustainable development of a culture characterized by shared leadership, a climate for learning and the communication of connections and high expectations.

## FOSTERING THE CAR CULTURE

> CAR has provided a pathway for teacher leadership within our school beyond the traditional leadership roles. CAR has provided teachers and school districts with a framework for teacher leadership that focuses on student achievement while also enhancing the culture of the school.
>
> —Laura Mathieu, Assistant Principal,
> Englewood Public Schools

Legendary management consultant, Peter Drucker, coined the phrase, "Culture eats strategy for breakfast," and nowhere do we see that more evident than in our school buildings today. Many a new principal has unwittingly focused on teacher "buy-in" as the means to the successful implementation of a new strategy or initiative with little to no regards for the prevailing school culture. Veteran teachers who have experienced a revolving door of "flavor of the month" programs throughout their careers have developed an instinctive "this too shall pass" response that is grounded in a long history of new approaches coming and going.

In the North Brunswick Public School District, implementation of the Connected Action Roadmap over the last five years has been the central framework for strengthening teaching, learning, and leading. Janet Ciarrocca, a former principal in the district and current Superintendent, notes, "[t]he schools in our district have been using the CAR framework to drive school improvement. Rather than looking at work on many different priorities as 'new initiatives,' the CAR framework connects them all together into one cohesive framework to drive school improvement efforts" (Ciarrocca, 2020, p. 84). Not only has CAR brought coherence across disparate strategies and initiatives, it has empowered the district to simultaneously work on building a more positive climate and culture while at the same time implementing structures and systems to strengthen teaching and learning. The outer triangle of the CAR diagram depicts the three core components of a strong school culture: (1) a climate for learning that includes all students and adults in the school building; (2) a culture of shared leadership that is authentic; and (3) the communication of connections and high expectations. As Ms. Ciarrocca states, "focusing on those three key cultural elements in your school can begin to build a strong foundation of a positive culture in which ALL stakeholders, both staff and students, are actively engaged in a culture of learning and working together for the best of the school" (Ciarrocca, 2020, p. 84).

In the North Brunswick school district, culture did not eat strategy for breakfast or lunch or dinner! Leaders at every level collaborated to build powerful learning communities that prevailed even as the schools shifted across virtual, in-person and blended learning environments in response to the pandemic. Strategically and directly addressing school culture through targeted professional learning communities, such as the School Climate Team (addressed in chapter 4), while at the same time improving the school climate through the daily work of PLCs engaged in collaborative conversations designed to strengthen teaching and learning creates a powerful combination for improving the learning environment.

## CAR LEADERSHIP ESSENTIALS: SHARED, DISTRIBUTED AND COLLABORATIVE

The CAR framework is built upon the foundational philosophy that leadership is not a solo activity, acknowledging the fact that individual administrators, alone, cannot improve teaching and learning. The CAR learning organizations that experience optimal results are those that genuinely embrace shared, distributed and collaborative leadership. As has been emphasized throughout this book, only through such leadership, mutual accountability and shared decision-making can administrators and teachers collectively and profoundly impact instruction across grade levels and content areas. Once achieved, the organizational culture shifts from a "my students" to an "our students" mindset. Those schools and districts that fail to recognize and "live" by this mantra, are simply not CAR learning organizations.

So, what does shared and distributed leadership look like in a CAR-driven learning organization? What does it mean to be a collaborative leader? To further capture the essence of CAR leadership across the learning organization and individual roles, consider the following definitions, descriptions and anecdotes.

### Shared Leadership

> Shared leadership can be defined as a dynamic interactive influencing process among individuals in groups for which the objective is to lead one another to the achievement of group or organisational goals or both. A key distinction between shared and traditional models of leadership is that the influence process involves more than just downward influence of subordinates by a positional leader. Leadership is distributed amongst a set of individuals instead of being centralised in the hands of a single individual who acts in the role of leader. (Pearce and Conger, 2002, p. 1)

As discussed earlier in this book, the most effective CAR leaders facilitate leadership in others and build the collective capacity for teaching, leading and learning. To achieve such, these leaders provide the time and structures for professional collaboration. The legitimate CAR leader respects and values teacher expertise and, as such, promotes professional learning communities as the decision-makers for curriculum, instruction, and assessment. All stakeholders in the school share in the leadership toward a single overarching goal—the destination—the optimal social, emotional, and academic learning of *every* student.

## Distributed Leadership

> Distributed leadership is primarily concerned with the practice of leadership rather than specific leadership roles or responsibilities. It equates with shared, collective and extended leadership practice that builds the capacity for change and improvement. . . . Distributed leadership means mobilising leadership expertise at all levels in the school in order to generate more opportunities for change and to build the capacity for improvement. The emphasis is upon interdependent interaction and practice rather than individual and independent actions associated with those with formal leadership roles or responsibilities. . . . Genuine distributed leadership requires high levels of trust, transparency and mutual respect. In very practical terms, to be most effective, distributed leadership has to be carefully planned and deliberately orchestrated. It won't just happen and if it does, there is no guarantee that it will have any positive impact. . . . When distributed leadership works well, individuals are accountable and responsible for their leadership actions; new leadership roles created, collaborative teamwork is the modus operandi and interdependent working is a cultural norm. Distributed leadership is about collective influence—it is not just some accidental by-product of high performing organizations but, as highlighted earlier, is a contributor to school success and improved performance. (Harris, 2014)

It is no secret that effective leadership is a hallmark of the highest performing schools. In fact, it is "second only to classroom instruction among school-related factors that affect student learning in school" (Wallace, 2011, p. 3). In a CAR learning organization, leadership is effectively distributed across all stakeholders—the Board of Education, the superintendent and central office, principal and assistant principal, and teachers. To this end, the Board of Education is deeply understanding of—and—fully committed to the CAR framework. Therefore, it establishes policies and aligns budgets in a way that ensures its comprehensive and sustained implementation. The district-level CAR Leadership Team, including the superintendent and central office, rely upon the CAR self-assessment rubric and related tools as a guiding influence of the district's strategic plan. Together, members of the district-level team utilize the CAR Rubric to conduct an initial baseline assessment, identify district priorities, formulate district-level action plans, formatively evaluate progress, and navigate continuous improvement on the path toward the ultimate destination—student learning.

Principals are responsible for providing the operational structures, managing school budgets, formally, informally, and empathetically observing and evaluating daily practice, and offering targeted feedback and sustained professional learning that strengthens the collective capacity of all educators. Additionally, building-level CAR Leadership Teams formulate action plans that are derived from the district's strategic- and/or CAR-specific plans, and effectively align to the unique needs of their respective school communities. Together, principals and teachers are the instructional leaders that comprise the professional learning communities—the driving force of

CAR. Each member of the PLC brings to it a unique skill set and experience, however, enthusiastically shares in the organizational vision, mission, and overarching goal—the continuous improvement of practice and individual student learning outcomes. Importantly, members of the PLC also equally contribute to the work.

## Collaborative Leadership

> By collaborative leadership, we mean the process of engaging collective intelligence to deliver results across organizational boundaries when ordinary mechanisms of control are absent. It's grounded in a belief that all of us together can be smarter, more creative, and more competent than any of us alone. . . . It calls on leaders to use the power of influence rather than positional authority to engage and align people, focus their teams, sustain momentum, and perform. Success depends on creating an environment of trust, mutual respect, and shared aspiration in which all can contribute fully and openly to achieving collective goals. Leaders must thus focus on relationships as well as results, and the medium through which they operate is high-quality conversation. (Oxford Leadership, 2017, p.3)

> To lead collaboratively is to lead through *conversation.* Collaborative leaders take personal responsibility for communicating effectively and consciously use focused, intentional conversation to achieve key ends. They cultivate the ability to communicate with presence and intention and use different modes of communication as required to support alignment, learning, or collective problem-solving and innovation...In a collaborative context, conversations have a different quality than they do in more hierarchical settings. Instead of being a medium for telling and directing, they serve as the vehicle for learning, co-creation, and collective achievement. (Oxford Leadership, 2017, p. 7)

As emphasized throughout this book, the signature attribute of the CAR framework is collaboration driven by meaningful conversations. As instructional leaders, the members of the grade-level and content area PLCs utilize the 10 Conversations (Appendix B) to organize, engage in and advance both practice and progress in learning. As was carefully examined throughout this book, these conversations provide the collaborative structure for the collective inquiry, data analysis, problem-solving and reflection essential to the PLC's efforts to develop, implement and continually revise and strengthen an equitable and viable curriculum that ensures individual student growth. Similarly, the 10 School Climate Team Conversations (Appendix L) guide the work of the School Climate Team to foster an optimal environment that supports both student and adult learning. Engaging consistently in the CAR conversations results in meaningful changes in professional practice and student outcomes within a strong collaborative culture.

# THE CAR AND A COMMON VISION FOR EDUCATION: ONE STATE'S SUCCESS STORY

> The Connected Action Roadmap has provided a common vision to drive the work of the Department of Education and has sent a strong message that focuses on building the capacity of every educator to provide equitable and targeted

instruction to every New Jersey student regardless of zip code. At the heart of the model is collaboration. With the support of all stakeholders and a common message, we are modeling strategies for working together and providing tools and support to enhance learning opportunities for all of New Jersey students as well as the educators and leaders who serve them.

—Former New Jersey Commissioner of Education,
Dr. Lamont Repollet, President of Kean University

Few—very few—education initiatives survive the many layers of institutional bureaucracy, let alone achieve the intended outcomes for positive gain. Ultimately, for such to occur it requires the individuals who lead these multiple and varied bureaucratic layers to genuinely embrace a shared vision and mission, one that is built upon the foundation of shared, distributed and collaborative leadership. From the grade-level PLCs, to district administrative teams, bargaining units and boards of educations, to county administrative offices and state agencies, each must be guided by a philosophy and framework that enables individuals to think, speak and act with unified purpose—student learning. Unlike the countless costly failing education initiatives that have come and gone with less than desired results, the Connected Action Roadmap has profoundly influenced educators and educational institutions. Why?

As has been amplified and exemplified throughout this book, CAR is not a program. It is not an initiative. It is not a step-by-step process that if you "just do this" you will experience student improvement. Rather, CAR represents the structures and processes needed to improve schools from within. CAR is an opportunity for schools to shift from a focus on compliance to a focus on practice and to set the foundation for a strong system of curriculum, instruction and assessment (Wright, 2019). Simply put, the CAR is a way of doing the business of education. More importantly, CAR is a way of doing the business of education *the right way.*

## The Partnership for Collaborative Learning

For far too long, the actions of educators have been reform driven. Reforms, in and of themselves, are not necessarily bad things. However, when they fail to put educators and students at the core and do not carefully consider the support necessary to yield meaningful changes to curriculum, instruction, and assessment, they actually *can* be bad things. As Michael Fullan (2011) explains in his article, "Choosing the Wrong Drivers for Whole System Reform," some policy and strategy levers should not be used as the first step in creating system-wide improvements.

Yes, of course, we should share accountability and ensure we have effective teachers in every classroom and effective leaders in every school. However, as we know all too well, education reform policies alone will not yield the desired results. For example, we cannot emphasize new standards and assessments as tools for accountability without supporting schools in their efforts to achieve meaningful change. If we do so, we ignore the very process that could ensure the accountability for the student learning we seek (Wright, 2019).

By 2018, the Connected Action Roadmap had established a reputation as a proven framework for school improvement in the state of New Jersey, so much so that a CAR-centric shared vision statement was formulated, adopted, and supported by the Partnership for Collaborative Professional Learning, a partnership of the major education organizations in New Jersey and the NJ Department of Education. These institutions clearly recognized the need for a common language and a coherent vision related to the practice of education. In 2019, the NJ Department of Education acted upon the CAR vision and initiated concrete steps to make the vision a reality across the NJ public schools. Why?

The Department understood that in order to advance practice and student learning in alignment to new standards and assessments, it would be essential to build the capacity of educators to develop, implement, reflect on and revise the curriculum, instruction and assessments they are using to ensure students meet the new standards. Furthermore, the Department recognized that when teachers are able to collaborate in effective PLCs and exchange best practices related to curriculum, instruction and assessment on a regular basis, it not only impacts the practice of one teacher, but enhances the instructional capacity of every teacher on the team—and across the school. Starting with a coherent vision encourages practitioners to consider the processes and structures that will support continuous growth, rather than encouraging the implementation of a myriad of seemingly unrelated initiatives that foster a sense of chaos and confusion.

The first step toward the realization of the shared statewide vision was to support all districts in implementing a strategic and collaborative approach to developing a standards-based curriculum that fosters equitable outcomes for all students. To this end, teams of educators from across New Jersey worked with the NJDOE Office of Standards and Assessment staff over several months to unpack the ELA and Math standards into clear specific learning goals and cluster them into suggested units of study. Ultimately, these units of study and related instructional resources would serve to increase the capacity to improve teaching and learning across NJ public school classrooms.

To further advance the Partnership for Collaborative Professional Learning's vision, grant-based programs were offered and funded through a partnership with the New Jersey Department of Education, the Overdeck Family Foundation, the Sands Foundation, and the Foundation for Educational Administration. The grant invited applications from NJ public school districts that were committed to utilizing selected grade levels of the newly released NJDOE Instructional Units in ELA and/or Math within the Connected Action Roadmap process. District applicants would need to embrace the overarching CAR-based goals of the initiative, specifically to:

1. Maintain a significant and consistent focus on PLC collaboration to improve instruction and student outcomes in professional learning community teams using the 10 CAR Conversations and the NJDOE Instructional Units.
2. Create a collaborative culture marked by a positive climate for learning for both students and adults, shared leadership, and a coherent approach to school improvement.

3. Assess the effectiveness of the use of common learning goals and PLC conversations to foster more effective collaborative analysis of formative assessment data that results in changes to instruction and improved student learning outcomes.
4. Assess the impact of leadership, both formal and informal, in sustaining the work.

In the end, numerous districts and schools across the state have institutionalized the CAR framework to establish a continuous cycle of school improvement and, most important, ensure that every student has access to a viable standards-based curriculum.

Advancing professional practice in our schools requires a shared vision, unified commitment, a collegial culture that embraces an "all for one and one for all" mindset, and a strategic systemic framework to support effective processes, all of which are cohesively driven by a single core purpose—individual student learning. While there may be other vehicles, CAR has proven to be successful on the journey toward the ultimate destination, a destination that is best captured by the renewed, post-pandemic shared vision statement of the Partnership found in Appendix R.

In the December 18, 2017, *Phi Delta Kappan* article, "Can Schools Meet the Promise of Continuous Improvement?," author Mark Elgart writes, "Continuous improvement is a journey that takes more time and greater effort from a wider range of stakeholders than most school initiatives. When implemented patiently, however, it enables schools to identify and meet all students' needs—which is the ultimate destination for all of us who have a stake in the future of our schools and our society" (Elgart, 2017, p. 59). And so, the author encourages all educators to join us on this journey of continuous school improvement, one that is driven by the CAR framework and, if fully embraced and institutionalized, is sure to get you to our ultimate destination—the optimal social, emotional, and academic learning of *every* student.

## REFERENCES

Ciarrocca, J. (Spring 2020). Culture eats strategy for breakfast. *Educational Viewpoints* 84. Retrieved from https://online.flipbuilder.com/iqbp/pzfg/mobile/index.html.

Dan, H. (2019, August 7). CAR curriculum units to be released soon – Pilot applications available. Retrieved November 15, 2021, from http://njpsa.org/car-curriculum-units-to-be-released-soon-pilot-applications-available

Elgart, M. (2017). Can schools meet the promise of continuous improvement? *Phi Delta Kappan* 99(4), 54–59.

Fullan, M. (May 2011). Choosing the wrong drivers for whole system reform. *Seminar Series Paper No. 204.* Retrieved November 15, 2021 from http://michaelfullan.ca/wp-content/uploads/2016/06/13396088160.pdf

Harris, A. (2014). Distributed leadership. *Teacher.* Retrieved November 16, 2021 from https://www.teachermagazine.com/au_en/articles/distributed-leadership

Learning Forward. (2011). Standards for professional learning. Retrieved November 10, 2021 from https://learningforward.org/standards-for-professional-learning/

Oxford Leadership. (2017). *White paper: Collaborative leadership.* Retrieved June 7, 2021 from https://www.oxfordleadership.com/collaborative-leadership

Pearce, C., and Conger, J. 2002. *Shared leadership: Underpinning of the MLCF*. Retrieved June 5, 2021 from https://www.leadershipacademy.nhs.uk/wp-content/uploads/2012/10/776bc9c27b6e8741d0ff42e593ba44cf.pdf

Wallace Foundation. (2011). *The school principal as leader: Guiding schools to better teaching and learning*. Retrieved from https://www.wallacefoundation.org/knowledge-center/Documents/The-School-Principal-as-Leader-Guiding-Schools-to-Better-Teaching-and-Learning.pdf

Wright, P. (Spring 2019). NJ embraces a common vision for strengthening teaching, leading and learning. *Educational Viewpoints* 4–8. Retrieved from http://online.flipbuilder.com/iqbp/ybwm/mobile/index.html#p=10.

# Appendix A

## *Summary of Roadblock and Forward Thinking*

| *ROADBLOCK THINKING* | *FORWARD THINKING* | *CHAPTER REFERENCE* |
|---|---|---|
| Principals can and should be direct instructional leaders. | Principals must empower those who directly impact student learning every day—the teachers. They are the direct instructional leaders. | Chapter 1 |
| If teachers use the curriculum documents created by a small group of teachers over the summer, they should be held responsible for ensuring student growth when students are assessed on grade-level standards. | If every teacher is responsible for student growth, then every teacher needs to engage in developing, implementing and revising a common master learning plan for the content and the students they teach. This will ensure that every teacher's practice is grounded in a viable curriculum marked by a tight alignment between grade-level standards, instruction and the assessments that will be used to measure student growth. | Chapter 2 |
| There is no problem if each teacher that teaches the same grade level and content creates their own learning objectives. | The creation of common SLOs is the foundation for equitable instruction. Common SLOs support the development of a common master learning plan and common assessments that lead to the effective collaborative analysis of student assessment data across a content area and grade level. | Chapter 2 |
| The review of individual weekly lesson plans by principals or supervisors ensures that all the components of the instructional plan are aligned to the standards. | Instructional Unit planning allows teachers to view the current learning in the context of the entire master learning plan. As the PLC revises and refines the plan based on student data they are continually adding to the repertoire of successful strategies and resources available for the varied learners in their classrooms. Because the unit plan is constructed horizontally, it allows both the teacher, and the supervisor that is monitoring instruction, to focus more clearly on alignment. The supervisor can also see how data analysis results in changes in the unit design. Discussion about these changes provides rich opportunities to strengthen the dialogue about teaching and learning between teachers and administrators. | Chapter 2 |

(Continued)

| ROADBLOCK THINKING | FORWARD THINKING | CHAPTER REFERENCE |
|---|---|---|
| If school teams and administrators review data from the classroom, district and/or state assessments, they are engaged in data-driven instruction. | Teacher-developed common formative and summative assessments provide immediate actionable data in relation to standards-aligned student learning objectives. Data-driven learning allows both teachers and students to utilize assessment feedback to make adjustments to the teaching and learning process. When data is collaboratively analyzed, teachers can utilize guiding questions to examine their practice and build on one another's strengths to better address student learning needs. | Chapter 2 |
| PLC practices have little impact on school climate. | Educators engaged in authentic collaboration related to student learning develop collective efficacy which in turn supports a positive climate for both student and adult learners. | Chapter 3 |
| Addressing negative adult behavior will only cause more problems. | By holding each other accountable for agreed-upon expectations in positive and assertive ways, educators reinforce the types of behaviors that will lead to a productive and collaborative professional learning environment. | Chapter 3 |
| There needs to be little alignment between the expectations for students and the expectations for adults. | Ensuring that expectations for students and adults are aligned supports students in building strong social and emotional learning skills. | Chapter 3 |
| There is little connection between a shared mission or vision, educator practice and a collegial climate. | A collaboratively developed student-focused mission statement built on shared beliefs and values is essential to creating a collaborative culture that strives to meet that mission daily. | Chapter 3 |
| School climate will fix itself. | School climate improvement requires a deliberate plan. | Chapter 4 |
| A positive school climate can be established by implementing a variety of programs and activities. | Schools need to implement a targeted and coherent school climate improvement plan. | Chapter 4 |
| Emphasis on academic achievement and assessment results means that teaching content knowledge and skills should take precedence over instruction in SEL. | Social and emotional learning results in higher levels of student achievement. Social and emotional instruction provides a foundation for safe and positive learning, and enhances students' ability to succeed in school, career, and life. | Chapter 4 |

# Appendix B

## *10 PLC Conversations*

### DEVELOPING, DELIVERING, REFLECTING, AND REVISING A COMMON MASTER LEARNING PLAN

1. Unpack content standards into clear, specific, student-friendly learning objectives (I Can or WALT—We are Learning To/That)
   - What is the student learning objective (SLO)? How does it relate to the standard? How will you communicate the goal to the students?
2. Cluster the standards and student-friendly learning objectives into instructional units
   - Are all learning goals taught and assessed in this unit?
3. Create essential questions
   - How can essential questions be used to provide a relevant purpose and engage students in their own learning? How will you use the essential questions during instruction or for assessment purposes?
4. Create summative assessments including rubrics, exemplars, and non-exemplars
   - Does your team agree on the criteria for success? What will provide evidence of learning? How have you determined the method of assessment and the level of rigor that the student must demonstrate based on the verbs used in the standards/SLOs? Are assessment tasks aligned to the SLOs? Does the summative assessment(s) assess all the SLOs in the unit? What learning goal does each assessment item assess?
5. Design pre-assessments and use data to inform instructional decisions
   - What are the prerequisite skills necessary as students begin their unit? What requisite skills and knowledge did you pre-assess?
   - What did the pre-assessment data tell you about each student's readiness to begin the unit? How will you differentiate based on this data? At what point in the unit will you need to provide differentiated instruction to certain individuals or groups of students? Do you need additional resources for reteaching or reach activities? Did the team find that students were particularly weak or strong in any prerequisite skills? Has this information been shared with previous grade-level teachers?

6. Design learning experiences including instructional activities, student strategies and formative assessments
   - What student strategies will support independent application of the skills and knowledge in this unit? What instructional activities and materials best align to the SLOs? What method are team members using to formatively assess the SLO(s) during instruction to make immediate changes in pace or lesson design?
7. Create common formative assessment benchmark tools for key points throughout the unit of study
   - At what point(s) in the unit will the team utilize a common benchmark assessment? What SLOs will be assessed at that point? Does the team agree on the criteria for success? What will provide evidence of learning? How have you determined the method of assessment and the level of rigor that the student must demonstrate based on the verbs used in the standards/SLOs? Are assessment tasks aligned to the SLOs? Can you involve students in peer or self-assessment? How will feedback be provided to students?
8. Analyze formative assessment data throughout the unit to drive instructional planning, differentiated activities and timely interventions
   - What did the common formative assessment tell you about each student's progress in mastering the SLOs? What type of differentiated activities and interventions can be provided for both struggling and high-achieving students based on the data? What did the data tell you about the instructional activities used in the unit thus far? Which ones were particularly successful or unsuccessful? How have unit plans changed to reflect the data? Did certain formative assessment methods provide more meaningful information about students' learning? How were the students involved in either peer or self-assessment? What feedback methods did you use? How did students respond to their feedback?
9. Analyze summative assessment data to evaluate student progress, revise unit learning experiences, revise unit assessments, seek targeted professional learning
   - What students are still struggling? What specific SLOs are they struggling with? How did these students perform on formative assessments of these SLOs during the unit? Are there any SLOs that the majority of students are still experiencing difficulty with? Are these prerequisite SLOs for other units of study? Could these SLOs be the target of SGOs next year? How will you continue to support these students in subsequent units?
   - How will the team improve either the unit or assessment design for next year? What resources do you need to improve the unit? What other teachers need the information from this summative assessment?
10. Discuss grading philosophy, policies, and procedures
    - What does 0 stand for? What is the purpose of homework? Can a student improve a grade if he/she uses teacher feedback or attends intervention, is reassessed and has met the goal? Does every member of the team grade the same way?

## CROSS-GRADE LEVEL AND CROSS-CONTENT CONVERSATIONS

How can we build knowledge and skills consistently across grade levels and content areas?

1. Ensure vertical alignment. Build upon prerequisite skills, increase expectations/rigor year to year.
2. Share student data with colleagues so they can better address students' needs.
3. Create ways to meaningfully integrate disciplines so students apply skills and knowledge from various content areas to solve a problem or create a product related to a real-world situation.
4. Share effective student strategies that can be used across grade levels and content areas.
5. Build a common language of learning.

# Appendix C
## *Unpacking a Standard Worksheet*

CONTENT STANDARD:

Knowledge/Concepts
What Do Students Need to Know/Understand?
Underline the Nouns

List Nouns:

| Skills<br>What Do Students Need to Be Able to Do?<br>Circle the Verbs<br>List Verbs: | Level of Bloom's Taxonomy<br>• Remember/Understand<br>• Apply/Analyze<br>• Evaluate/Create |
|---|---|

Student-Friendly Learning Objectives Aligned to This Standard:

# Appendix D

## *CAR Instructional Unit Template*

| Unit Title:<br><br>Grade Level:<br><br>Timeframe: |
| --- |
| Essential Questions |
| |
| Standards |
| Standards (Taught and Assessed): |

| Instructional Plan | | | | |
|---|---|---|---|---|
| Pre-assessment | | | | |
| SLO – WALT We are learning to/ that | Student Learning Strategies | Formative Assessment | Activities and Resources | Reflections & Modifications (ELL, Special Education, Gifted, At-risk of Failure, 504) |
| | | | | |
| | | | | |
| | | | | |
| | | | | |
| | | | | |
| Common Formative Assessments: | | | | |
| | | | | |
| | | | | |
| | | | | |
| Summative Assessments | | | | |
| | | | | |

# Appendix E

## *Guide to Developing the CAR Instructional Unit Plan*

Unit Title:

Grade level:

Time frame:

Essential Questions

Questions that reveal the big ideas underlying the unit content. Essential questions allow students to better understand why the learning in this unit is important and how it is connected to other learning and to real-world applications.

Standards

Standards (Taught and Assessed)

Instructional Plan

Pre-Assessment

Pre-Assessment

Assess students' mastery of prerequisite skills required for this unit. Assess key requisite skills. Reflect on data to determine key decisions related to differentiating instructional plan.

| Student Learning Objectives (SLO)—WALT | STUDENT STRATEGIES | FORMATIVE ASSESSMENT | ACTIVITES AND RESOURCES | MODIFICATIONS AND REFLECTIONS |
|---|---|---|---|---|
| We are learning to (refers to a skill or strategy)<br>We are learning that (refers to a concept) | STUDENT STRATEGIES are:<br>• A means to an end<br>• Approaches *students* might use to achieve the student learning objective<br>• A set of steps likely to lead students to successful engagement in their own learning | FORMATIVE ASSESSMENT refers to the ongoing process students and teachers engage in when they:<br>• Focus directly on the SLO(s)<br>• Take stock of where current work is in relation to the SLO(s)<br>• Provide feedback so the student can take action to move closer to mastery | ACTIVITIES are the instructional models and teaching strategies teachers will use that most effectively align with the specific student learning objectives (SLO—WALT). | MODIFICATIONS are the methods teachers use to make learning accessible to all students.<br>They *do not* change the WALT (SLO) but rather provide different pathways to achieving the specified SLO. |

| | | | | |
|---|---|---|---|---|
| | STUDENT STRATEGIES are very different from *teaching strategies* in that they are modelled by teachers and used independently by the students to support their learning and *apply what they have learned.*<br>EXAMPLES:<br>General Learning—Example: Active Listening<br>• Look at the person who is speaking.<br>• Think about what they are saying.<br>• Restate what they said.<br>Ask clarifying questions.<br>EXAMPLES – cont'd: Subject Specific – Example:<br>RACE Method:<br>1. Restate the question<br>2. Answer the question<br>3. Cite evidence from the text<br>4. Examples and Evidence from the text to support your answer<br>Calculate Area of Triangle:<br>1. Identify and measure the base and height.<br>2. Multiply the base by the height.<br>3. Divide by 2.<br>4. Record the units in squares. | FORMATIVE ASSESSMENTS<br>**Temperature Checks—Occurs during the lesson*—Immediate, in the moment assessments that give a sense of current student status and allow the teacher to adjust pace or content. For example, Thumbs up, thumbs down, use of whiteboards, questioning<br>**Break Points*—Quick assessments at the end of a lesson or two that allow the teacher to make instructional decisions about how to proceed. For example, Exit slips, quick quiz, quick written explanations<br>*proceed. For example, Exit slips, quick quiz, quick written explanations<br>• * *Student Self and Peer Assessments*—Self evaluative<br>student reflections that allow the student to set goals for moving to mastery.<br>• * Common *Formative Assessments*—These common formative assessments should be placed at key points in the unit to check mastery of several SLOs. These assessments should be developed in alignment with the SLOs that have been taught. Data will be analyzed by the PLC in order to make unit revisions, and plan for differentiated instruction<br>Timely and targeted feedback is the key to students' use of formative assessment: information<br>Making targeted instructional decisions and taking action is the key for teachers. Data should result in adjustments to instructional practice. | RESOURCES are the materials, visuals, online sources, supplies, and so on, that are best suited to support the attainment of the SLO | REFLECTIONS: This can also be used as a place to jot down notes about unit design. What went well? What should the PLC consider changing? |

# COMMON FORMATIVE ASSESSMENT(S)

| Common Formative Assessment | Modifications and Reflection |
|---|---|
| Common Formative *Assessments*—These should be placed at key points in the unit. These common formative assessments are given after several lessons to check mastery of several SLOs. These assessments should be developed in alignment with the SLOs that have been taught. Data can be analyzed by the PLC in order to make unit revisions, and plan for differentiated instruction | MODIFICATIONS are the methods teachers use to make assessments accessible to all students.<br>REFLECTIONS: This can also be used as a place to jot down notes about assessment design. What did student performance tell us about aspects of the unit or aspects of the assessment design? What should the PLC consider changing? |

Common Summative Assessments

| Common Summative Assessments | Modifications and Reflections |
|---|---|
| Common summative assessments are given at the end of the unit to evaluate students' progress in achieving the standards. There can be more than one assessment and varied types of assessments, that is, multiple-choice, open-ended, performance, project, and so on. The PLC collaboratively creates the assessment(s) ensuring alignment to the SLOs. | MODIFICATIONS are the methods teachers use to make assessments accessible to all students.<br>REFLECTIONS: This can also be used as a place to jot down notes about assessment design. What did student performance tell us about aspects of the unit or aspects of the assessment design? What should the PLC consider changing? |

# Appendix F

## *The Important Role of Classroom Assessments and Common Assessments*

Throughout the CAR instructional unit, assessment development, implementation, and analysis inform educators of their impact on students' learning, their next steps in instruction and students' next steps in learning through ongoing teacher feedback.

### CONVERSATION 4: QUESTIONS AFTER A PRE-ASSESSMENT

1. Which students in each class need to work on prerequisite skills and concepts? What skills? What concepts? What does this mean for unit planning? How will we address these gaps?
2. What misconceptions are evident in student responses?
3. Which students in each class have the mastered requisite skills? What skills? What does this mean for unit planning? What types of extension activities need to be developed?
4. What learning goals do we need to focus on during whole group instruction?
5. Is the pre-assessment effectively measuring student mastery of the prerequisites and requisites? Does it need revisions? Are the questions and/or tasks aligned to the SLOs? Are the directions clear?

### CONVERSATION 6: TYPES OF FORMATIVE ASSESSMENT BUILT INTO LEARNING EXPERIENCES

- *Temperature Gauges*: Immediate, in-the-moment assessments that give a sense of current student status and allow the teacher to adjust the pace or modify the content
- *Break Points:* Quick assessments at strategic points that allow the teacher to step back and revise the next steps in instruction
- *Student-Directed Assessments*: Peer and self-assessments that give both the student and teacher insight related to individual progress toward mastery of learning goals

## CONVERSATION 7: QUESTIONS AFTER A COMMON FORMATIVE ASSESSMENT

1. With which SLOs are most students struggling? What do their responses tell us about their misconceptions or misunderstandings?
2. What reteaching strategies and activities will be used with these students?
3. With which SLOs are students most successful? What do their responses tell us?
4. Which students need reinforcement or reach activities?
5. What strategies and activities will we develop for those students?
6. What additional instructional resources do we need to meet the learning needs of our students?
7. What does the data tell us about our instruction? What needs to change? What can we learn from one another?
8. How can the data be shared with students to encourage reflection, goal setting and ownership for learning?
9. Is the common formative benchmark assessment effectively measuring student achievement of the standards? Does it need revisions? Are the questions and/or tasks aligned to the SLOs? Are the directions clear?

## CONVERSATION 8: QUESTIONS AFTER A COMMON SUMMATIVE ASSESSMENT

1. With which SLOs are most students struggling? What do their responses tell us about their misconceptions or misunderstandings?
2. With which SLOs are students most successful? What do their responses tell us?
3. What interventions were used throughout the unit with the students who were struggling on the common formative assessment(s)? Did those students continue to make the same errors?
4. Will these SLOs be addressed again? In what unit? How will we strengthen that unit to reinforce skills and concepts for specific students? Are these SLOs prerequisite skills for future units? Which ones? How will we differentiate instruction in those units to support individual students?
5. What other teachers need this information?
6. What does the data tell us about our instruction? What needs to change? What can we learn from one another?
7. What professional resources or professional learning opportunities do we need to assist us in strengthening this instructional unit?
8. Is the summative assessment effectively measuring student mastery of standards? Does it need revisions? Are questions and tasks aligned to the SLOs? Are directions clear?

# Appendix G

## *Professional Expectations of Educators at School*

1. Focus on student learning
2. Help one another and accept help
3. Share ideas and materials
4. Be objective
5. Have a sense of humor
6. Be viable resources for each other
7. Be team players
8. Offer and accept constructive criticism
9. Respect ourselves and each other
10. Be sensitive and non-judgmental
11. Actively listen to one another
12. Set high expectations for students and one another
13. Be willing to compromise
14. Refrain from gossip
15. Recognize that everyone has a voice
16. Use I statements to foster positive communication
17. Be positive and assume positive intent
18. Be flexible
19. Share accountability and responsibility for student learning
20. Hold each other accountable for meeting our agreed-upon expectations

# Appendix H

## *Group Norms Reflection*

**HOW ARE WE DOING?**

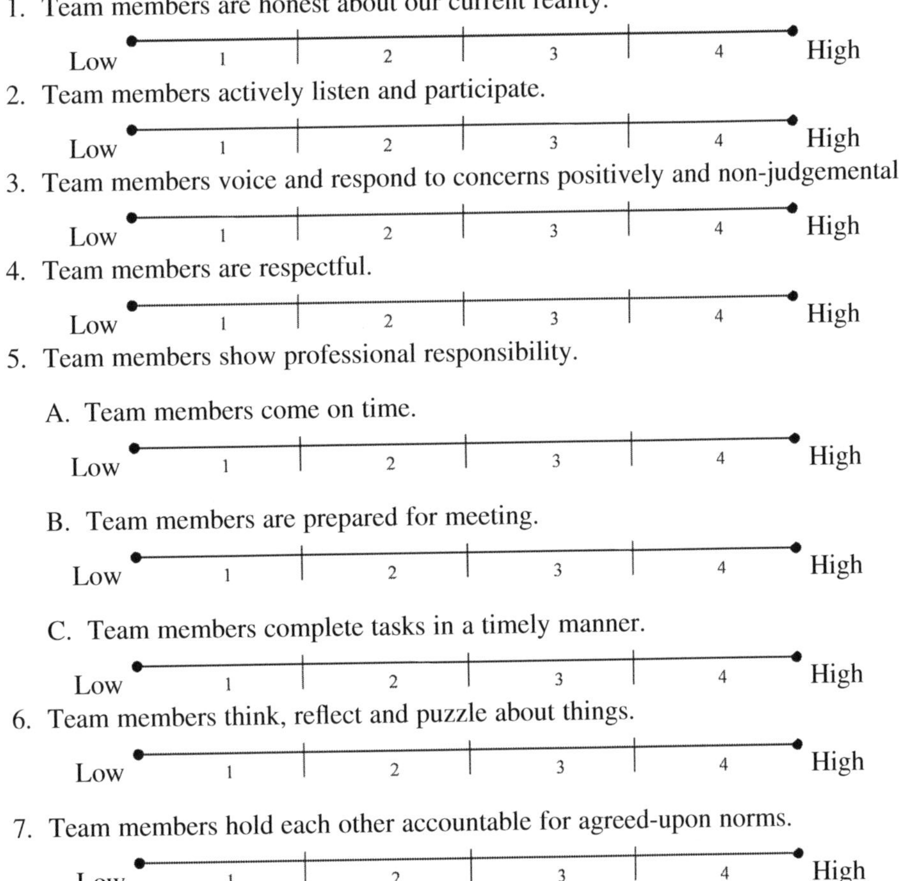

1. Team members are honest about our current reality.

   Low 1 2 3 4 High

2. Team members actively listen and participate.

   Low 1 2 3 4 High

3. Team members voice and respond to concerns positively and non-judgementally

   Low 1 2 3 4 High

4. Team members are respectful.

   Low 1 2 3 4 High

5. Team members show professional responsibility.

   A. Team members come on time.

   Low 1 2 3 4 High

   B. Team members are prepared for meeting.

   Low 1 2 3 4 High

   C. Team members complete tasks in a timely manner.

   Low 1 2 3 4 High

6. Team members think, reflect and puzzle about things.

   Low 1 2 3 4 High

7. Team members hold each other accountable for agreed-upon norms.

   Low 1 2 3 4 High

# Appendix I

## *Individual Norms Reflection*

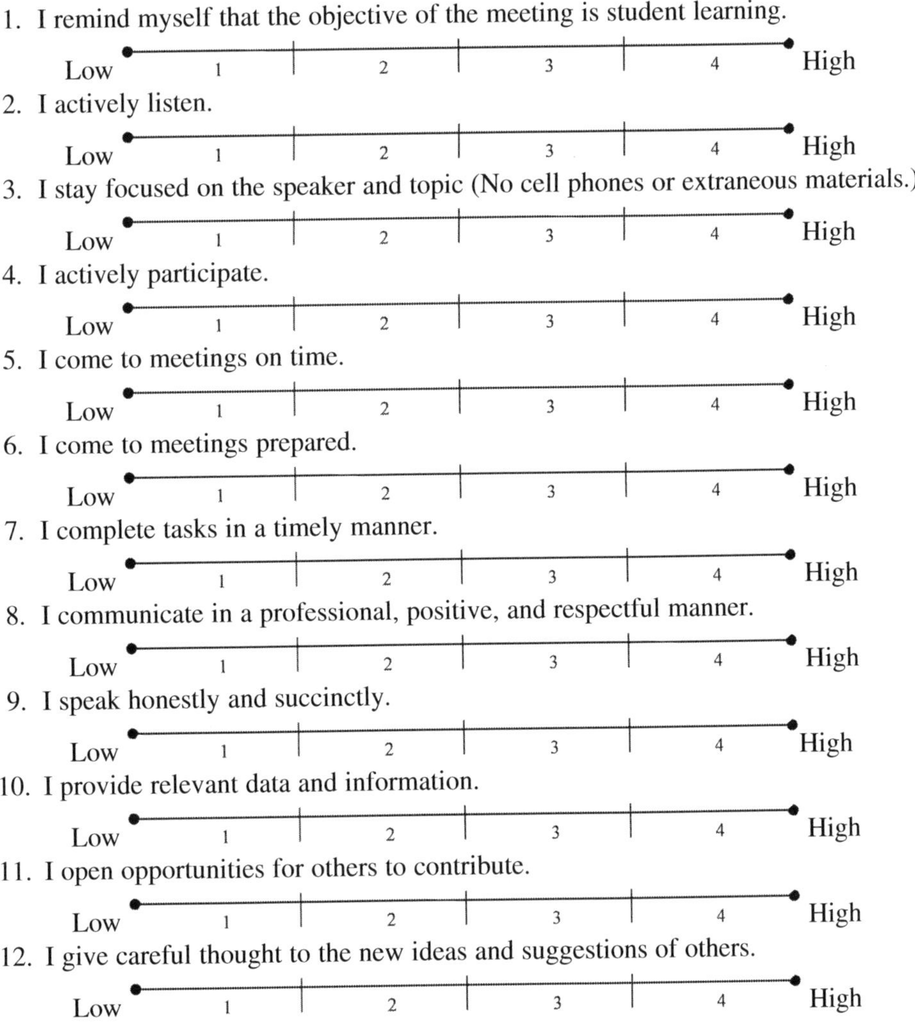

1. I remind myself that the objective of the meeting is student learning.

   Low 1 2 3 4 High

2. I actively listen.

   Low 1 2 3 4 High

3. I stay focused on the speaker and topic (No cell phones or extraneous materials.)

   Low 1 2 3 4 High

4. I actively participate.

   Low 1 2 3 4 High

5. I come to meetings on time.

   Low 1 2 3 4 High

6. I come to meetings prepared.

   Low 1 2 3 4 High

7. I complete tasks in a timely manner.

   Low 1 2 3 4 High

8. I communicate in a professional, positive, and respectful manner.

   Low 1 2 3 4 High

9. I speak honestly and succinctly.

   Low 1 2 3 4 High

10. I provide relevant data and information.

    Low 1 2 3 4 High

11. I open opportunities for others to contribute.

    Low 1 2 3 4 High

12. I give careful thought to the new ideas and suggestions of others.

    Low 1 2 3 4 High

13. I hold myself accountable to the norms.

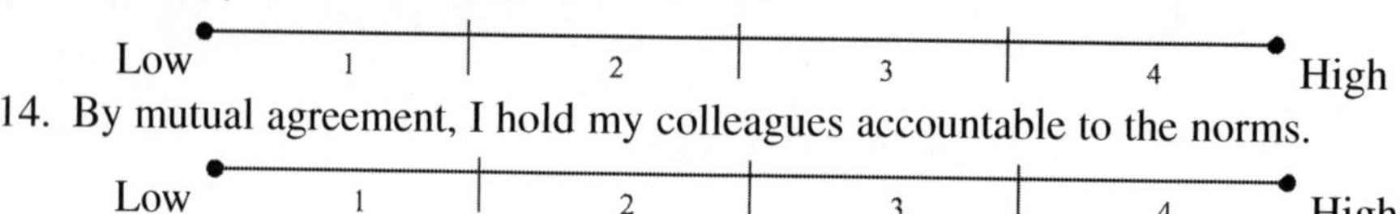


14. By mutual agreement, I hold my colleagues accountable to the norms.

# Appendix J

## *Mission Statement*

**REVISED**

_______________________________School is a community of learners.

The mission of the school is to ensure that all students meet and exceed the NJ Student Learning Standards, develop the six pillars of character, and develop the skills necessary to be lifelong learners and productive citizens in the twenty-first century.

Pillars of Character: Trustworthiness, respect, responsibility, fairness, caring, and citizenship

We believe:

1. All students are unique and can learn
2. Students learn best in a safe, caring, and motivating environment that is based on mutual respect
3. Students can apply learning strategies and utilize self-assessment tools to take ownership for their learning
4. Students can develop critical, creative, problem-solving, and decision-making skills
5. Students can develop the pro-social skills necessary to ensure a respectful and collaborative learning environment
6. Students can develop the pillars of character through opportunities for action in the school and community
7. Optimum learning occurs when teachers communicate learning goals to students and parents and support their achievement through standards-based instruction and ongoing assessment
8. It is the responsibility of the administration and the Board of Education to provide the leadership, support, and provide the resources necessary to achieve our mission
9. All members of the school community must model the pillars of character
10. It is the responsibility of the school community to inspire students to reach their highest potential and to value lifelong learning

We value:

1. A strong home-school connection
2. A standards-based curriculum
3. Differentiated instruction
4. Formative and summative assessment
5. The development of student strategies for independent learning and the application of skills and knowledge
6. Shared responsibility and accountability
7. Collaboration and communication
8. Shared leadership
9. Job-embedded professional learning that creates a consistency and continuity of instruction across grade levels and content areas
10. Active participation of all stakeholders in the community of learners

Our mission will become a reality when it is supported by actions that are driven by our beliefs and our values.

# Appendix K

## *The Professional Climate: What Is Our Current Reality?*

**TABLE APPENDIX K.1**

| Adult Climate<br>1. Civil<br>2. Congenial<br>3. Contrived Collegial<br>4. Collegial | Professional Expectations | Aligned Expectations Student/Adults | Shared Mission | Shared Leadership | The Real Work of PLCs | Coherence |
|---|---|---|---|---|---|---|
| MY SCHOOL | | | | | | |

Adult Climate:
Circle the descriptor that best describes your current professional climate:

Civil: Adults fail to consistently demonstrate strong interpersonal skills and have limited opportunity for engagement with one another.
Congenial: Adults demonstrate positive social relationship skills. This climate is marked by a "we all get along" mentality.
Contrived Collegial: In contrived collegial environments, professionals are engaged in PLCs in name only. Their collaborative work lacks a clear purpose and a strong connection to their daily practice. This causes educators to view their so-called teamwork as a "waste of time."
Collegial: Professionals are committed to working together to ensure that all students learn. Structures are place to support authentic collaboration, professional discourse and job-embedded professional learning

Professional Expectations:

1. Low: Clear professional expectations have not been discussed or established or the administration has set the professional expectations.
2. Moderate: The staff has engaged in a discussion about professional expectations leading to the collaborative establishment of a common list of expectations.

Accountability for meeting those expectations has not been discussed and is not evident.

3. High: The staff has collaboratively developed professional expectations. All staff hold each other accountable for meeting the expectations.

Aligned Expectations for Behavior for Students and Adults

1. Low: There are no clear expectations established for students and/or adults.
2. Moderate: There are clear expectations for student behavior and adult behavior. Some adults model the expectations to reinforce appropriate behavior.
3. High: Adult expectations are aligned to expectations for students and the majority of the staff is committed to continuous reinforcement of both sets of expectations through daily interactions with students and modeling of appropriate behavior.

Shared Mission

1. Low: A mission statement has not been developed or it has been developed by the administration. It is not utilized to drive school improvement.
2. Moderate: The staff has collaboratively developed a shared mission built on shared values and beliefs. The mission is used infrequently to drive school improvement discussions.
3. High: The staff has collaboratively developed a shared mission based on beliefs and values. The mission is used to drive our collective work. It is revised based on new understandings that lead to the development of additional values and beliefs.

Degree of Shared Leadership:

1. Low: There is little or no shared responsibility and accountability. The formal leader may consult with a select group of teachers.
2. Moderate: The principal seeks input from teachers during the decision-making process. The formal leadership encourages teachers to take on leadership roles.
3. High: Leadership is shared resulting in shared responsibility and shared accountability. There is open communication and when problems arise, solutions are sought through collective inquiry. There are numerous opportunities for teachers to assume leadership roles. The school is driven by a "We are in this together" philosophy.

The Real Work of PLCs

1. Low: PLC teams are not in place or PLC teams operate in name only to meet QSAC compliance. Most teachers think they are a waste of time.
2. Moderate: Teachers meet in grade-level PLC teams to discuss lesson activities and share resources. There is a lack of structure and focus at team meetings. There is little analysis of student work and if it is analyzed, the discussion does not result in changes to the curriculum, instruction, or assessment.

3. High: The focus of PLC work is student learning. PLC teams have established norms to ensure meetings are productive. Teams engage in collaborative planning of instruction, analysis of student formative and summative assessment data, and the sharing and development of instructional strategies to meet common learning goals. Curriculum and assessments are consistently revised based on the conversations of the PLC teams. PLC outcomes have a direct impact on teacher practice and student learning.

Coherence

1. Low: The school suffers from initiative fatigue mostly because stakeholders look outside themselves for answers. There is little conversation about the reasons for a new initiative and even less about the need for follow-through and the impact on student learning.
2. Moderate: The school is subject to initiative fatigue because expectations are not clear and connections are weak. Conversations may occur about why there is a need for this initiative or program, but there are few structured conversations to provide feedback during its implementation. Parents and students often are out of the loop when it comes to understanding why new approaches are taken. Methods for evaluating the effectiveness of the initiative are weak or unclear.
3. High: New initiatives are examined in the light of how they will impact student learning. Careful consideration is given to how a new initiative will be implemented and what student data will be used to assess its impact. Collaborative conversations take place before and during implementation so adjustments can be made based on timely data. Leadership communicates the reason for implementation, ongoing progress, and results to all stake.

# Appendix L

## *10 School Climate Team Conversations*

Assessing, Planning, Implementing, and Reflecting on a Coherent Approach to School Climate Improvement

1. Create a common language. What is school climate? What is our vision of a positive school climate?
2. Assess our current reality. What initiatives/programs are currently in place to address the various dimensions of school climate? What is the goal of the program/initiative? What evidence do we have that the goal is being met?
3. Identify student learning objectives related to social and emotional learning. What do we want students to know, understand and be able to do in terms of social and emotional learning? What skills can we teach schoolwide? How will these skills positively impact relationships in the school? Who will teach the students these skills? How will they be taught and consistently reinforced? How will schoolwide social and emotional learning objectives connect to the school and classroom code of conduct?
4. How would we describe the climate for learning for adults? Do professionals have clear expectations for collegial behavior? Does staff model the social and emotional learning skills that are taught to students? Are there opportunities for collaborative professional learning?
5. Identify assessment data. What assessment tools will be used to assess the dimensions of school climate? What other data is already available?
6. Analyze assessment data and any other available school data to drive the development of a coherent school climate improvement plan.
7. Develop a coherent plan that includes specific actions, anticipated results, and identifies the evidence of success.
8. Focus on communication and community engagement. How and when will the plan be communicated? How will staff, students, parents, and community members be involved in the development, implementation, and assessment of the plan?
9. Implement the plan and use formative data to make necessary adjustments.
10. Analyze summative data, reflect and revise action plans.

## Key Ideas to Consider

- Communicate all plans, actions, and the resulting data with all stakeholders with a strong emphasis on "why" the actions are being taken and what role each stakeholder plays in implementation.
- Build a common language related to behavioral expectations and social and emotional learning.
- Choose a limited number of social and emotional learning skills related to building positive relationships as the focus for schoolwide lessons.
- Ensure everyone is involved in teaching and reinforcing the schoolwide lessons.
- Create ways to meaningfully integrate social and emotional learning into the curriculum across grade levels and content areas.
- Share effective strategies and instructional activities and resources that can be used across grade levels and content areas.
- Make strong connections between the expectations for students and the expectations for adults.
- If there are multiple schools in the district, plan opportunities to meet and share ideas and resources in order to create a comprehensive district-wide approach to building a climate for learning.
- Don't forget to celebrate. Celebrations build community.
- Involve students – school climate is a shared responsibility. Once they value the positive climate, they will protect and sustain that climate.
- Be a model PLC – set norms, adhere to them, and focus on the continuous cycle of climate improvement.

# Appendix M

## *The 14 Dimensions of School Climate Measured by the CSCI*

### BY THE NATIONAL SCHOOL CLIMATE CENTER AT RAMAPO FOR CHILDREN

*The 14 Dimensions of School Climate Measured by CSCI*, National School Climate Center for Children at Ramapo, 2021, NSCC Online. https://schoolclimate.org/wp-content/uploads/2021/08/CSCI-14-Dimensions-Chart.pdf//www.schoolclimate.org

| DIMENSIONS | MAJOR INDICATORS |
|---|---|
| SAFETY | |
| 1. Rules and Norms | Clearly communicated rules about physical violence; clearly communicated rules about verbal abuse, harassment, and teasing; clear and consistent enforcement and norms for adult intervention. |
| 2. Sense of Physical Security | Sense that students and adults feel safe from physical harm in the school. |
| 3. Sense of Social-Emotional Security | Sense that students feel safe from verbal abuse, teasing, and exclusion. |
| TEACHING AND LEARNING | |
| 4. Support for Learning | Use of supportive teaching practices, such as encouragement and constructive feedback; varied opportunities to demonstrate knowledge and skills; support for risk-taking and independent thinking; atmosphere conducive to dialogue and questioning; academic challenge; and individual attention. |
| 5. Social and Civic Learning | Support for the development of social and civic knowledge, skills, and dispositions including effective listening, conflict resolution, self-reflection and emotional regulation, empathy, personal responsibility, and ethical decision making. |
| INTERPERSONAL RELATIONSHIPS | |
| 6. Respect for Diversity | Mutual respect for individual differences (e.g., gender, race, culture, etc.) at all levels of the school—student-student; adult-student; adult-adult, and overall norms for tolerance. |

(Continued)

| | |
|---|---|
| 7. Social Support—Adults | Pattern of supportive and caring adult relationships for students, including high expectations for students' success, willingness to listen to students and to get to know them as individuals, and personal concern for students' problems. |
| 8. Social Support—Students | Pattern of supportive peer relationships for students, including friendships for socializing, for problems, for academic help, and for new students. |
| INSTITUTIONAL ENVIRONMENT | |
| 9. School Connectedness/ Engagement | Positive identification with the school and norms for broad participation in school life for students, staff, and families. |
| 10. Physical Surroundings | Cleanliness, order, and appeal of facilities and adequate resources and materials. |
| 11. Social Inclusion | Acceptance of students with disabilities as members of the school community, including enhanced opportunities for socialization, extracurricular activities, leadership, and decision-making. |
| SOCIAL MEDIA | |
| 12. Social Media | Sense that students feel safe from physical harm, verbal abuse/teasing, gossip, and exclusion when online or on electronic devices (e.g., Facebook, Twitter, and other social media platforms, by an email, text messaging, posting photo/video, etc.). |
| STAFF ONLY | |
| 13. Leadership | Administration that creates and communicates a clear vision, and is accessible to and supportive of school staff and staff development. |
| 14. Professional Relationships | Positive attitudes and relationships among school staff that support effective working and learning together. |

# Appendix N

## *The CAR Planning Guide*

| | |
|---|---|
| Leadership Teams | Is our district and/ or school CAR Leadership Team representative of all stakeholders? Does everyone on the team have an understanding of the CAR framework? |
| PLCs | Are grade-level/content area PLCs currently in place? Do PLCs have consistent, protected time during the school day to engage in the 10 CAR Conversations? |
| Curriculum | How is the curriculum currently developed? How will that process shift to the work of PLCs and the design of instructional units? |
| Roadblock and Forward Thinking | Review the *Summary of Roadblock and Forward Thinking* (Appendix A). What examples of Roadblock Thinking are currently accepted in our district/school? What Forward Thinking do we want to consistently message to stakeholders? |
| Vision Setting | How does CAR support our vision for strengthening teaching, leading, and learning? Why do we want to implement CAR? What are our desired outcomes? |
| Self-Assessment | CAR Leadership Team members should individually complete the CAR Rubric (Appendix P). As a group discuss the ratings and determine priorities for each CAR element. When will others be given the opportunity to engage in the rubric assessment? How will we use the results? |
| Implementation Plan | What is our plan? CAR is a journey, therefore a multi-year plan is needed. Once the major goals of the multi-year plan are established, create a detailed action plan for Year 1 that includes each step of the plan, the timeline and the necessary resources. Once the plan is in place, how will we continue to monitor and adjust as needed? |
| Roles | Review the *Leadership Roles Within CAR* Tool (Appendix S). What are the responsibilities of the various leadership positions in our district/school in CAR implementation and sustainability? |
| Communication | How will the CAR Vision and the implementation plan be shared? How will educators be introduced to CAR in order to gain an understanding of the process? |

(Continued)

| | |
|---|---|
| Professional Learning | What professional learning and/or coaching will be provided to educators in order to deepen their understanding of CAR and the 10 CAR Conversations? What professional learning will support school/district leaders in CAR implementation? |
| Culture | What areas of adult climate will need to be addressed in order for grade-level/content area PLC teams to be most effective? When will School Climate Teams be established? How will their work be supported? |

# Appendix O

## *The CAR Rubric*

### SUPPORTING A CYCLE OF CONTINUOUS SCHOOL IMPROVEMENT

| *Element: Standards, SLOs, and Effective Instruction* | *Not Addressed* | *Emerging* | *Developing* | *Sustaining* |
|---|---|---|---|---|
| Focus on Student Learning | We have not agreed upon a set of guiding questions that will help create a common focus on student learning. | We have adopted a set of guiding questions to focus our conversations on student learning. | We have adopted a set of guiding questions and key conversations and are beginning to collaboratively address the questions in our PLC teams. | Our PLC teams regularly address a set of guiding questions by engaging in key conversations. Answers to the questions are reflected in our instructional units |
| Standards and Student Learning Objectives | We have not unpacked the standards into clear, specific, student-friendly learning objectives (SLOs). | We have started to unpack the standards into clear student learning objectives (SLOs). | We have unpacked the standards into SLOs and have developed instructional units that clearly communicate which SLOs will be taught and assessed in each unit | We consistently implement, revise, and reflect on SLOs as we deliver our instructional units. We assess students to determine their progress in meeting those SLOs and use the data to drive changes in instruction and unit design. |

| *Element: Standards, SLOs, and Effective Instruction* | *Not Addressed* | *Emerging* | *Developing* | *Sustaining* |
|---|---|---|---|---|
| Alignment | We have not aligned standards, student learning goals, instructional models/student strategies/ activities/ resources, formative assessments, summative assessments, and instructional activities. | We have aligned our SLOs to the standards and have begun to collaboratively build instructional units by developing assessments and instructional models/student strategies/ activities/ resources that are aligned to those SLOS | We have aligned all components of our instructional units | We have aligned all components of our instructional units. We consistently use student data results to reflect on and revise all components to ensure tight alignment |
| Effective Instruction | We have not worked collaboratively to determine which instructional models/student strategies/activities and resources will engage students and enable them to master specific SLOs | We have shared some instructional models/student strategies/activities and resources that we feel will help students master specific SLOs | We have collaboratively analyzed student data and discussed which instructional models/ student strategies/ activities and resources contributed to successful student outcomes | We consistently share and model instructional models student strategies/activities and resources that contribute to successful student outcomes based on the ongoing collaborative analysis of formative and summative assessment data. The most effective instructional elements are embedded into our units of study. |
| Social and Emotional Learning (Curriculum Embedded) | We have not identified the SEL competencies appropriate to embed into our instructional units. | We have identified the SEL competencies appropriate to embed into our instructional units. We have developed SLOs for our grade level/content area based on the competencies | We have identified the SEL competencies appropriate to each unit. We have developed SLOs and embedded them into the instructional units where they will be taught and assessed | We consistently implement, revise, and reflect on SLOs aligned to the SEL competencies. We assess students to determine their progress in meeting those SLOs, and use the assessment data to drive changes in instruction and unit design |

| *Element: Assessment* | *Not Addressed* | *Emerging* | *Developing* | *Sustaining* |
|---|---|---|---|---|
| Summative Assessments | We have not developed common summative assessments | We have begun to develop common summative assessments for specific instructional units | We have developed common summative assessments for some instructional units and we collaboratively analyze student summative data to determine student progress in mastering the SLOs for those units | We have developed common summative assessments for all instructional units. We collaboratively analyze student summative data to determine student mastery, plan next steps in instruction, and reflect on and revise unit instruction and/or assessments |
| Pre-Assessments | We have not developed common pre-assessments. | We have begun to develop common pre-assessments for specific instructional units | We have developed common pre-assessments for some instructional units and we collaboratively analyze student pre-assessment data to determine student mastery of requisite and prerequisite SLOs | We have developed common pre-assessments for all instructional units. We collaboratively analyze student pre-assessment data to determine student mastery of requisite and prerequisite SLOs. We use this data to form flexible groups and develop differentiated learning opportunities |
| Formative Assessments | We do not utilize formative assessments to determine student progress in meeting SLOs | We use formative assessments to determine student progress in meeting SLOs during daily instruction. We have not developed common formative assessments to administer at key points in the unit | We consistently use formative assessments to monitor student progress during daily instruction. We have developed common formative assessments to administer at key points in the unit. We record formative assessment data and provide specific feedback to students. The formative assessment drives the next steps in instruction for teachers and allows students to make adjustments to their learning | We consistently use formative assessments to monitor student progress during daily instruction. We have developed common formative assessments to monitor the progress of each SLO in a unit. We collaboratively analyze the results of common formative assessments and plan next steps for instruction including, differentiation and intervention. Students are provided targeted feedback, differentiated learning opportunities, and appropriate targeted interventions. We reassess to determine the success of interventions. Successful differentiated activities and intervention strategies are embedded into instructional units |

| *Element: PLC* | *Not Addressed* | *Emerging* | *Developing* | *Sustaining* |
|---|---|---|---|---|
| Teams/Focus/ Goals | We are not organized into collaborative teams. | We are organized into collaborative teams, but we are not working on goals that are directly related to student learning | We are organized into collaborative teams that work interdependently on common goals directly related to student learning | We are organized into collaborative teams that focus their work on common goals directly related to student learning. The results of the ongoing analysis of student assessment data drive the work of our collaborative teams in achieving those goals |
| Time | We are not provided time for collaborative job-embedded professional learning. | We use available after-school meeting time for collaborative job-embedded professional learning. | We are provided at least one period a week of common planning time to focus on collaborative job-embedded professional learning. | We are provided common planning time at least three times a week for collaborative job-embedded professional learning. We also utilize available after-school meeting time and in-service days. Time is also provided within the school day to meet and/or observe colleagues as needed |
| Norms | We have not developed team norms | We have developed team norms | We have developed team norms and review those norms before each meeting | We have developed team norms and review the norms before each meeting. We periodically assess team adherence to the norms and consistently address violations of the norms to ensure that we are focused on student learning in an efficient and productive manner |
| Conflict | We do not have an agreed-upon method of resolving conflicts | We have discussed how we will resolve conflicts in our team. | We have established an agreed-upon method of resolving team conflicts, but do not consistently confront conflict and apply that method. | We have established and consistently apply an agreed-upon method of resolving team conflicts. We understand that conflict can be productive if handled openly and resolved with a focus on what is best for student learning |

| Element: Teacher and Principal Effectiveness | Not Addressed | Emerging | Developing | Sustaining |
|---|---|---|---|---|
| Connection between Student Learning and Educator Evaluation | Research-based evaluation frameworks are not utilized to evaluate teachers and principals. Little feedback is provided during the evaluation process. There is no connection between evaluation and professional learning | Research-based evaluation frameworks are utilized to evaluate teachers and principals. All teachers and leaders have received sufficient training in the evaluation frameworks. We have begun to create a common language about effective teaching and leading. Feedback is provided after each formal evaluation. There is little connection between evaluation and professional learning | Research-based evaluation frameworks are utilized to evaluate teachers and principals. The evaluation frameworks for teachers and leaders are aligned and we have created a common language about teaching and leading. All teachers and leaders have received sufficient training in the evaluation model. Meaningful feedback is provided after most formal and informal observations. The feedback includes connections to the instructional units that not only informs individual practice but also informs the conversations of the PLC. Professional improvement plans are linked to individual needs identified through the evaluation process | Aligned research-based evaluation frameworks are utilized to evaluate teachers and principals. The components of our instructional units and the elements of our evaluation frameworks have created a common language and context for effective teaching and leading. All teachers and leaders have received sufficient training in the evaluation frameworks. Evaluation outcomes are used to not only improve individual practice but to focus on building collective efficacy. Evaluation outcomes are used to not only improve individual practice but to focus on collective efficacy. The data also informs unit revisions. Meaningful feedback is provided after all informal and formal observation. Professional improvement plans are linked to both individual needs identified through the evaluation process and PLC team goals. Instructional units provide the context for applying the elements of effective practice. Team collaboration strengthens the professional practice of all members |

| Element: Culture | Not Addressed | Emerging | Developing | Sustaining |
|---|---|---|---|---|
| School Climate Team | We have not established a shared leadership team to focus on developing, fostering and maintaining a positive school climate for both students and adults | We have established a shared leadership team to focus on developing, fostering, and maintaining a positive school climate for both students and adults | We have established a shared leadership team to focus on developing, fostering and maintaining a positive school climate for both students and adults. The team includes varied stakeholders and meets at least monthly. We have utilized key school climate team conversations to drive the development of a school climate team improvement plan. To ensure student voice and engagement, we invite students to join in the conversations where appropriate. We use some school climate data to derive the development of the school climate improvement plan | We have established a shared leadership team to focus on developing, fostering and maintaining a positive school climate for both students and adults. The team includes varied stakeholders and meets at least monthly. We have utilized key school climate team conversations to drive the development of a school climate team improvement plan. To ensure student voice and engagement, we invite students to join in the conversations where appropriate. We consistently use a variety of school climate data to drive the development and ongoing revision of the school climate improvement plan |
| Clear Expectations for Student Behavior | We have not established clear expectations for student behavior. | We have established clear expectations for student behavior. Expectations are not reinforced consistently. Discipline is not fairly and consistently applied | We have established clear expectations for student behavior. Expectations are reinforced consistently. Discipline is fairly and consistently applied | We have established clear expectations for student behavior that are part of a larger plan to address students' social and emotional learning and character development. The expectations are connected to the student code of conduct. Teachers have collaboratively established consistent and grade-appropriate classroom rules that are aligned with the school's code of conduct |

| Element: Culture | Not Addressed | Emerging | Developing | Sustaining |
|---|---|---|---|---|
| Social and Emotional Learning (School wide) | We have not identified SLOs in the area of SEL to drive school-wide instruction with a focus on developing positive relationships | We have identified SLOs for SEL that are taught to all students with a focus on developing positive relationships. They are taught by a designated staff member | We have identified SLOs for SEL that are taught to all students with a focus on developing positive relationships. All staff has been trained and a majority of professional staff are responsible for teaching-related lessons | We have identified SLOs for SEL that are taught to all students with a focus on developing positive relationships. All staff has been trained and all members of the professional staff are responsible for teaching and reinforcing the lessons, creating a common language related to SEL. Parents are trained in the lessons so they can be reinforced at home. PLC grade-level/ content area teams also integrate SEL competencies into their instructional units in a purposeful way that ensures assessment of SEL objectives |
| Social Environment – Students | Interactions among students and adults are often marked by disrespect. Students frequently experience teasing, bullying or exclusion. There is little tolerance for diversity and differences. There is little sense of belonging. Celebrations are rare. Students are not engaged in | Some interactions among students and adults are marked by respect. Students sometimes experience teasing, bullying or exclusion. There is some degree of tolerance for diversity and differences. There is some sense of community and belonging. Celebrations are held once or twice a year. Some students are engaged in extra-curricular, service learning or community-related activities | The majority of interactions among students and adults are marked by respect. Students have been taught social skills that help them successfully interact with both students and adults. Students infrequently experience teasing, bullying or exclusion and have been taught what to do in situations of normal conflict and bullying. Tolerance for diversity and differences is taught in most classes. There is a sense of community and belonging on the part of both students and | Mutual respect is one of the core values and is an expectation that has been clearly communicated to all stakeholders. Members of the school community hold each other accountable to meet this expectation. Students have been taught social skills that help them successfully interact with both students and adults. Adults model these skills in their interactions with both students and adults. Students infrequently experience teasing, bullying or exclusion, and have been taught what to do in situations of normal conflict and bullying. There is evidence that |

| Element: Culture | Not Addressed | Emerging | Developing | Sustaining |
|---|---|---|---|---|
| | extra-curricular, service learning or community-related activities | | staff. Celebrations are held throughout the school year to build school spirit. Students have an opportunity to take on leadership roles in planning and implementing school climate initiatives. Most students are engaged in extra-curricular, service learning or community-related activities | students apply these skills which are reinforced throughout the school year. Tolerance for diversity and differences is the focus of classroom and school-wide initiatives. Diversity and differences are viewed as strengths of the school community. There is a strong sense of community. All stakeholders feel a part of the school community. Celebrations are held throughout the year. Celebrations are purposeful and occur to send a bigger message that is related to school climate goals. Celebrations involve all stakeholders. Students have an opportunity to take on leadership roles in planning and implementing school climate initiatives. The majority of students are engaged in extra-curricular, service learning or community-related activities |

| Element: Culture | Not Addressed | Emerging | Developing | Sustaining |
|---|---|---|---|---|
| Physical Environment | Physical spaces are not conducive to learning. School safety and emergency plans are not communicated clearly to all staff | Some physical spaces are inviting and conducive to learning. School safety plans have been developed and clearly communicated to some staff. | The school has a physical environment that is conducive to learning. School plans have been developed in coordination with local police and clearly communicated to all staff. Parents and community members are aware that the school has plans that ensure the protection of all students | The school has a physical environment that is conducive to learning. Student work is displayed and there is an inviting feeling when parents and community members enter. School plans have been developed in collaboration with local police and clearly communicated to all staff. These plans are reviewed regularly and adjusted based on drill outcomes or other data. Parents and community members are aware that the school has plans and that they are consistently revised and updated to ensure the protection of all students. The local police have a positive relationship with students and staff and they participate in school community activities. |
| Rules/ Norms: Students | School and classroom rules are not effectively communicated. Consequences are not clear and are not given consistently | School rules are well communicated to all stakeholders. Consequences are clear and are sometimes given consistently | School and classroom rules are clear and aligned and are communicated to all stakeholders. Consequences are clear and are given consistently | School and classroom rules are clear and consistent with our core values and our SEL goals. All rules are communicated to all stakeholders. Consequences are clear and are given consistently. Emphasis is on discipline as a learning tool. Discipline related conversations reinforce SEL/CD goals |

| Element: Culture | Not Addressed | Emerging | Developing | Sustaining |
|---|---|---|---|---|
| Teaching and Learning | There is little student engagement in learning. There is little differentiation of instruction. Students do not feel challenged academically. Struggling students do not feel supported. There is no effective intervention system. Students do little collaborative work and do little peer and self-assessment. Students rarely set their own learning goals | Students are sometimes engaged in learning. Teachers sometimes differentiate instruction to ensure they meet the needs of all learners. Formative assessment and feedback are sometimes used to support student learning. Interventions are not provided consistently. Students sometimes work collaboratively and sometimes engage in peer and self-assessment. Students sometimes set their own learning goals | Students are frequently engaged in learning. Teachers frequently differentiate instruction based on formative assessment data. Students are provided with appropriate and timely feedback to enhance their ability to achieve learning objectives. There is a tiered intervention system in place. Students frequently work collaboratively and frequently engage in peer and self-assessment. Students frequently set their own learning goals. | Students are active partners in their learning. Teachers regularly differentiate instruction. Students are provided with appropriate and timely feedback to enhance their ability to achieve the learning objectives. Students feel ownership for their learning and often take initiative to ask questions and seek assistance as needed. Students support one another and have regular opportunities to peer and self-assess. Students regularly set their own learning goals based on these assessments. |

| Element: Culture | Not Addressed | Emerging | Developing | Sustaining |
|---|---|---|---|---|
| Programs/ Initiatives Approaches (PIA) Related to School Climate | We do not have programs, initiatives, or approaches (PIA) that are directly related to a school climate improvement plan | We have several PIA to support school climate improvement. Initiatives seem somewhat connected and purposeful. Leadership sometimes communicates the importance of embracing the new PIA. There is little ongoing support for new programs. There is little communication about how PIA are directly connected to a coherent school climate improvement plan. Buy-in is weak | We have established PIA to address specific school climate improvement goals. Our school community often understands why we are engaging in the PIA. Sometimes programs are modified to ensure they meet the needs identified in the School Climate Improvement plan. There is some ongoing support for PIA but implementation is inconsistent. An evaluation of the program/practice is sometimes conducted to determine effectiveness. Buy-in is moderate | We have established PIA to address specific school climate improvement goals. We communicate the purpose and connections between goals and PIA to all stakeholders to create a coherent approach to climate improvement. Leadership monitors the consistent implementation of any program or practice. During implementation, feedback in the form of formative student/ climate data is used to modify PIA as necessary to ensure they meet specific needs addressed in the School Climate Improvement Plan. We assess the effectiveness of all initiatives and communicate the findings to all stakeholders. Buy-in is strong |

| Element: Culture | Not Addressed | Emerging | Developing | Sustaining |
|---|---|---|---|---|
| Mission | We do not have a shared mission | We have collaboratively developed a shared mission | We have collaboratively developed a mission built on shared values and beliefs that contain references to the components of school climate | We have collaboratively developed a mission built on shared values and beliefs that contain references to both academic and SEL. Our mission statement communicates where we want to go and how we will get there. We use our mission statement to drive our collective work. We revise the mission statement at least yearly based on new understandings of the practices that bring us closer to achieving the mission. The mission has been well communicated to all stakeholders |
| Collegial Environment | Adult relationships are generally civil. Incidents frequently occur that demonstrate a lack of mutual respect. We do not regularly share our professional knowledge. It is easier to avoid conflict than confront issues that are barriers to creating a focus on student learning | Adult relationships are generally civil. Some teachers have developed congenial relationships. Most staff members respect one another, but we do not have a structure to regularly share professional knowledge. It is easier to avoid conflict than confront issues that are barriers to creating a focus on student learning | Adult relationships are generally congenial. Some teachers have developed more collegial relationships by consistently sharing professional knowledge in PLC teams. There is a general feeling of mutual respect. Some staff feel comfortable addressing conflict and voicing concerns | Adult relationships are collegial. We have the structures in place that allow educators to regularly exchange professional knowledge. There is an agreed expectation that we treat each other with mutual respect. We have an agreed-upon method of resolving conflict and reaching consensus |

| Element: Culture | Not Addressed | Emerging | Developing | Sustaining |
|---|---|---|---|---|
| Clear Expectations for Professional Behavior | We have not established clear expectations for professional behavior. There is little connection between the expectations for adult and student behavior. | We have developed a set of expectations for professional behavior. The connections between the expectations for adult behavior and student behavior is weak. | We have collaboratively developed a set of expectations for professional behavior. Formal leaders hold colleagues accountable for meeting those expectations. We have discussed the connection between the behavior of adults and the behavior of students | We have collaboratively developed a set of expectations for professional behavior. We hold each other accountable for meeting those expectations. We consistently address behaviors that detract from our focus on student learning. There is a strong connection between the expectations for student and adult behavior. |
| Shared Leadership | Leadership is hierarchical. There is a divide between formal leaders and staff. There is little shared responsibility and accountability | Leadership is limited to formal leaders or shared with a small group of people. Attempts are made to engage more teachers in decision making. Limited opportunities exist to take on leadership roles | Formal leaders provide opportunities for teachers to demonstrate leadership. The leader consistently engages teachers in decisions and encourages them to take on both formal and informal leadership roles | Leadership is shared. Every professional shares responsibility and accountability for student learning. There are numerous opportunities for teachers to demonstrate leadership. Practices and processes that drive higher levels of student learning can be sustained over time because they are not dependent upon a single or small group of leaders |

| Element: Culture | Not Addressed | Emerging | Developing | Sustaining |
|---|---|---|---|---|
| Communication of Connections Across the System | We are suffering from initiative fatigue. Programs and initiatives are disjointed. We consistently look outside ourselves for answers to identified problems. There is no ongoing support for new programs. There is little buy-in because the majority of staff members have a "this too shall pass" attitude | Initiatives seem somewhat connected and purposeful. Leadership sometimes communicates the importance of embracing new practices and/or programs. There is little ongoing support for new programs. New programs are not modified to meet our students' specific needs. Buy-in is weak because some staff do not believe the change will be sustained | A needs assessment process is used to identify areas of concern. Leadership works collaboratively with stakeholders to identify possible solutions. Our school community often understands why we are engaging in new programs/practices. Sometimes programs are modified to ensure they meet the needs of our students. There is some ongoing support for new initiatives, but implementation is inconsistent. An evaluation of any new program/practice is sometimes conducted to determine effectiveness | Needs are identified through the collaborative analysis of student data. Solutions are developed collaboratively. Programs and best practices are modified as necessary to ensure they meet our students' specific needs. The CAR framework is used to communicate how decisions about engaging in any new programs or practices strengthen components of the roadmap. Leadership consistently communicates the connection between the new practice and our mission. Leadership monitors the consistent implementation of any new program or practice. During implementation, feedback in the form of student data is used to determine the effectiveness |
| School Climate Data Collection and Analysis | We do not collect or analyze data related to school climate | We collect data related to school climate | We collect data related to school climate and analyze the data collaboratively to drive yearly school climate improvement plan development | We collect both formative and summative data related to school climate. We analyze the data throughout the year to drive school climate improvement plan development, reflection and revision |
| School Climate Improvement Plan | We do not develop a school climate plan | We develop a yearly school climate plan | We develop a yearly school climate improvement plan that includes specific goals based on the analysis of school climate data. The plan is shared with stakeholders | We develop a school climate improvement plan that includes specific measurable goals that are based on the analysis of school climate data. The plan is shared with stakeholders. Updates are provided regularly on progress in plan implementation |

# Appendix P

## *Crosswalk: Standards for Professional Learning Summary and the CAR*

Standards for Professional Learning (revised 2022) at https://learningfaorward.org

| Frame | Standards Statements | Key Concepts | Connected Action Roadmap (CAR) |
|---|---|---|---|
| Rigorous Content for Each Learner | Equity Practices<br>Professional learning results in equitable and excellent outcomes for all students when educators understand their students' historical, cultural, and societal contexts, embrace student assets through instruction, and foster relationships with students, families, and communities. | • Educators understand students' historical, cultural, and societal contexts.<br>• Educators embrace student assets through instruction.<br>• Educators foster relationships with students, families, and communities. | • Use common Diversity, Equity and Inclusion (DEI) language in PLCs to support equitable curriculum units.<br>• Support the collective efficacy of staff to ensure PLCs assess their strengths and weaknesses to support equitable learning and assess student learning needs. |
| | Curriculum, Assessment, and Instruction<br>Professional learning results in equitable and excellent outcomes for all students when educators provide high-quality curriculum and instructional materials for students, assess student learning, and understand curriculum and implement through instruction. | • Educators provide high-quality curriculum and instructional materials.<br>• Educators assess student learning to advance progress.<br>• Educators understand curriculum and implement it through instruction. | • Support the development of PLC knowledge and skills in creating a viable curriculum.<br>• Develop common standards-based instructional units within PLCs.<br>• Ensure alignment of SLOs, student and instructional strategies, and assessments in the development and delivery of instructional units.<br>• Use data analysis protocols of formative and summative assessment results to improve student access to mastery of grade-level standards. |
| | Professional Expertise<br>Professional learning results in equitable and excellent outcomes for all students when educators apply standards and research to their work, develop the expertise essential to their roles, and prioritize coherence and alignment in their learning. | • Educators apply relevant standards and research.<br>• Educators strengthen discipline-specific expertise.<br>• Educators sustain coherence and alignment. | • Use a continuous improvement process that is driven by ten specific conversations.<br>• Support staff collective accountability and learning of student standards and research-based instructional practices.<br>• Use educator performance standards to enhance both individual and collective educator practice through PLC conversations and collegial support such as peer observation and coaching.<br>• Use the PLC as the vehicle for the development and implementation of a viable curriculum. |

| *Frame* | *Standards Statements* | *Key Concepts* | *Connected Action Roadmap (CAR)* |
|---|---|---|---|
| Transformational Processes | Equity Drivers<br>Professional learning results in equitable and excellent outcomes for all students when educators prioritize equity in professional learning practices, identify and address their own biases and beliefs, and collaborate with diverse colleagues. | • Educators prioritize equity in professional learning practices.<br>• Educators identify and address their own biases and beliefs.<br>• Educators collaborate with diverse colleagues. | • Collaborate to create and implement a school mission focused on creating a healthy culture focused on equitable learning processes.<br>• Provide ongoing opportunities to revisit and reflect on beliefs and principles that support all learners.<br>• Engage in "unpracticed conversations" to build capacity for supporting student agency and choice. |
| | Evidence<br>Professional learning results in equitable and excellent outcomes for all students when educators consider evidence and data from multiple sources, use data to plan and monitor learning, and assess the impact of professional learning on educators and students. | • Educators consider evidence and data from multiple sources.<br>• Educators use data to plan and monitor learning.<br>• Educators assess the impact of professional learning on educators and students. | • Ensure that data analysis from a comprehensive assessment system results in changes in instructional practice and improvement of student learning outcomes.<br>• Demonstrate the impact of PLC actions on teacher and leader practice and student learning.<br>• Provide the mechanism to identify the targeted professional learning needs of educators. |
| | Learning Designs<br>Professional learning results in equitable and excellent outcomes for all students when educators set relevant and contextualized learning goals, ground their work in research and theories about learning, and implement evidence-based learning designs. | • Educators set relevant and contextualized learning goals.<br>• Educators ground their work in research and theories about learning.<br>• Educators implement evidence-based learning designs. | • Actively engage educators in learning that is immediately applied to classroom instruction.<br>• Use student standards to set PLC goals and outcomes for high-quality instruction.<br>• Provide and model protocols that promote educator collaborative inquiry, reflection and innovation. |
| | Implementation<br>Professional learning results in equitable and excellent outcomes for all students when educators understand and apply research on change management, engage in feedback processes, and implement and sustain professional learning. | • Educators understand and apply research on change management.<br>• Educators engage in feedback processes.<br>• Educators implement and sustain professional learning. | • Focus on a sustained and reflective implementation process for an aligned curriculum for all students.<br>• Provide critical feedback to colleagues throughout the teaching and learning cycle.<br>• Drive the need for change through the ongoing analysis of student data.<br>• Create coherence that supports a sustained focus on educator practice and student learning. |

(Continued)

| Frame | Standards Statements | Key Concepts | Connected Action Roadmap (CAR) |
|---|---|---|---|
| Conditions for Success | Equity Foundations<br>Professional learning results in equitable and excellent outcomes for all students when educators establish expectations for equity, create structures so that all staff members have access to learning, and sustain a culture of support for all staff. | • Educators establish expectations for equity.<br>• Educators create structures so that all staff have access to learning.<br>• Educators sustain a culture of support for all staff. | • Collaboratively develop staff and student expectations for a robust system of learning.<br>• Plan for and implement professional learning structures focused on curriculum, assessment and instruction.<br>• Provide ongoing supports for all staff to build their capacity for teaching and learning processes. |
| | Culture of Collaborative Learning<br>Professional learning results in equitable and excellent outcomes for all students when educators commit to continuous improvement, build collaboration skills and capacity, and share responsibility for improving learning for all students. | • Educators commit to continuous improvement.<br>• Educators build collaboration skills and capacity.<br>• Educators share responsibility for improving learning for all students. | • Move educators to more effective practice while moving students to mastery of content standards through the CAR conversations.<br>• Align educator standards, student learning standards and professional learning standards.<br>• Engage in the PLC process and practices that support the tight connection between teacher collaboration, curriculum and classroom instruction. |
| | Leadership<br>Professional learning results in equitable and excellent outcomes for all students when educators establish a compelling and inclusive vision for professional learning, ensure a coherent system of support to build individual and collective capacity, and advocate for professional learning by sharing the importance and evidence of impact of professional learning with others. | • Educators establish a compelling vision for professional learning.<br>• Educators sustain coherent support for professional learning.<br>• Educators advocate for results-oriented, evidence-based professional learning. | • Support the district mission and vision through targeted professional learning.<br>• Develop capacity for shared instructional leadership.<br>• Support continuous job-embedded professional learning focused on student learning.<br>• Ensure that PLC s are structured in a way that they become the foundational support system. |

| *Frame* | *Standards Statements* | *Key Concepts* | *Connected Action Roadmap (CAR)* |
| --- | --- | --- | --- |
| | Resources<br>Professional learning results in equitable and excellent outcomes for all students when educators allocate resources for professional learning, prioritize equity in their resource decisions, and monitor the use and impact of resource investments. | • Educators allocate and coordinate resources for professional learning.<br>• Educators prioritize equity in their resource decisions.<br>• Educators monitor the use and impact of resource investments. | • Build human capital by enabling collegial sharing of best practices related to curriculum, instruction and assessment.<br>• Prioritize and protect regularly scheduled time for job-embedded professional learning community work.<br>• Use resources, including technology, in a targeted way to enhance teaching and learning. |

# Appendix Q

## *Leadership Roles within CAR*

### SUPERINTENDENT

- Establishes and facilitates a vision for a systemic approach to continuous district improvement focused on student learning that strengthens Collaborative Professional Learning
- Promotes a district culture that supports collaboration
- Works collaboratively with district and school-based leaders to ensure an effective PLC process
- Provide time and structures for collaborative collegial conversations related to curriculum, instruction, and assessment
- Ensures cross-district articulation of best practices
- Ensures that a comprehensive assessment system includes the collaborative analysis of both formative and summative data
- Promotes shared leadership and shared responsibility that supports the development of leadership at every level

### DIRECTOR OF CURRICULUM AND INSTRUCTION

- Establishes and facilitates a systemic approach to continuous district improvement focused on student learning that strengthens Collaborative Professional Learning
- Promotes a district culture that supports collaboration
- Works collaboratively with district and school leaders to ensure an effective PLC process
- Shares leadership to build mutual accountability and responsibility for student learning by supporting the growth of teacher leadership
- Provide time and structures for collaborative collegial conversations related to curriculum, instruction, and assessment
- Ensures that a comprehensive assessment system includes the collaborative analysis of both formative and summative data
- Ensure the collaborative development and implementation of viable, standards-aligned curricula that include: common, student learning objectives; valid, reliable,

assessments; a variety of challenging, engaging and effective instructional strategies and practices; and appropriate levels of targeted and timely interventions
- Provides multiple opportunities for building leaders to collaboratively develop and deliver professional learning and share their best practices across the district

## SUPERVISOR

- Sets clear expectations for professional behavior that emphasize and support professional collaboration
- Celebrates success and provides opportunities to share best practices across the district
- Shares leadership to build mutual accountability and responsibility for student learning by supporting the growth of teacher leadership
- Works collaboratively with district and school leaders to ensure an effective PLC process
- Ensures the collaborative development and implementation of viable, standards-aligned curricula that include: common, student learning objectives; valid, reliable, assessments; a variety of challenging, engaging and effective instructional strategies and practices; and appropriate levels of targeted and timely interventions
- Facilitates district-wide PLC meetings of teacher leaders to ensure the collaborative development of a viable, standards-aligned curriculum
- Leads collaborative analysis of district-wide assessment data with district teams to determine how the results of data analysis will change practice and improve student
- Provides collaborative, job-embedded professional learning opportunities and resources that will allow teachers to develop valid, reliable, well-aligned assessments, use effective protocols to analyze data, and share their best practices

## PRINCIPAL

- Establishes and facilitates a systemic approach to continuous school improvement focused on student learning that strengthens Collaborative Professional Learning
- Promotes a school culture that supports collaboration
- Works collaboratively with district and school leaders to ensure an effective PLC process.
- Shares leadership to build mutual accountability and responsibility for student learning by supporting the growth of teacher leadership
- Sets clear expectations for professional behavior that emphasize and supports professional collaboration
- Celebrates success and provides opportunities to share best practices within the school and across the district
- Provide time and structures for collaborative collegial conversations related to curriculum, instruction, and assessment
- Ensures, through observation, review of unit plans, and ongoing dialogue with PLC teams, that teachers: (1) develop well-structured lessons with common,

standards-based SLOs, (2) develop valid, reliable, well-aligned assessments; and (3) employ a variety of challenging, engaging, and effective instructional strategies and practices so that all students are taught a standards-based curriculum and receive appropriate levels of targeted and timely intervention.

- Monitors changes in practice and student learning resulting from the work of PLC teams that is focused on curriculum, instruction, and assessment
- Regularly reviews common formative and summative assessment data and has follow-up discussions with teachers and PLCs
- Provides collaborative, job-embedded professional learning opportunities and resources that will allow teachers to develop valid, reliable, well-aligned assessments, use effective protocols to analyze data, and share their best practices

## TEACHER LEADER

- Facilitates PLC meetings
- Ensures that PLCs have established norms, for which they hold each other accountable, to guide their professional work
- Models clear expectations for professional behavior that emphasize and support professional collaboration
- Leads collaborative discussions related to developing, implementing, reflecting on, and revising a well-aligned curriculum
- Leads collaborative analysis of formative and summative unit data using effective protocols with school-based PLC teams
- Leads dialogue to determine how the results of data analysis will change practice and improve student learning
- Works with other PLC team leaders to ensure both horizontal and vertical articulation
- Provides opportunities for shared leadership of the PLC team to support the growth of teacher leadership
- Works collaboratively with school and district leaders to ensure an effective PLC process

# Appendix R

## *Statement of Vision and Commitment*

### CONNECTED ACTION ROADMAP: A SYSTEMS APPROACH TO STRENGTHENING TEACHING, LEADING, AND LEARNING

The major New Jersey educational organizations seek to ensure equitable access to high-quality education and post-secondary success for all students. We value a strategic and collaborative approach that connects standards-based curriculum, instruction, assessment and professional learning in a school culture that promotes an ongoing process of reflection on and growth in student learning. We commit to strengthening teaching, leading, and learning by supporting districts to:

- develop a viable standards-based curriculum that directly informs classroom instruction and assessment;
- create a comprehensive assessment system that includes ongoing formative and summative assessments resulting in data that informs practice and drives student learning;
- promote a shared understanding of effective teaching, leading, and learning that informs job-embedded professional learning;
- operate as professional learning communities characterized by strong collaboration, shared leadership with a focus on curriculum, instruction, and assessment; and
- foster a climate for student and adult learning marked by mutual respect, shared leadership, and high expectations for every student.

We believe that, in the post-pandemic environment, reaffirming a comprehensive statewide commitment to these principles will empower NJ educators to continue to meet the needs of all students now and in the future across multiple learning environments. We remain committed to engaging as collaborative partners to ensure that New Jersey's standing as a national leader in educational practice is sustained.

Endorsed Partnerships:

- American Federation of Teachers New Jersey
- Garden State Coalition of Schools
- Learning Forward
- New Jersey Association of Colleges for Teacher Education
- New Jersey Association of School Administrators
- New Jersey Association of Supervision and Curriculum Development
- New Jersey Education Association
- New Jersey Parent Teachers Assocation
- New Jersey Principals and Supervisors Association
- New Jersey School Boards Association
- The Foundation for Educational Administration
- The Madison Institute Education

# About the Contributors

Donna McInerney, Ed.D.
Donna McInerney currently serves as the chief executive officer of the Foundation for Educational Administration, the professional learning division of the New Jersey Principals and Supervisors Association (NJPSA). A former high-school teacher and supervisor, she has spent most of her career at the secondary and post-secondary levels, having taught in the Department of Graduate Education, Leadership and Counseling Program at Rider University and in the Secondary Education Preparation Program at The College of New Jersey.

Throughout the course of her career, Donna has presented at state and national conferences on instructional leadership, collaborative learning communities, research-based instructional strategies, and the Connected Action Roadmap (CAR). Supporting educators to strengthen teaching, learning, and leading represents Donna's passion and the driving force behind her work.

Brian Chinni, Ed.D.
Brian has served the educational profession for over 30 years as a teacher, school principal, district-level administrator, university professor, graduate program director, associate dean, and entrepreneur. In 1999, Brian established the Madison Institute (TMI), a New Jersey-based educational consultant and professional development firm serving K-12, higher education, and government agencies, both at home and abroad. Since its inception, TMI, under Brian's leadership, has been integrally involved in many important federal- and statewide educational collaborative initiatives with the New Jersey Department of Education, many national state-based superintendents, principals, and supervisors associations, numerous school districts and consortia throughout the state and the northeast, institutions of higher learning, and international ministries of education.

In addition, Brian joined Ramapo College of NJ in 2008 as the director of the Master of Arts in Educational Leadership (MAEL) program, and professor of Educational Leadership. He currently serves as the assistant dean of Teacher Education and Certification Program and MAEL program director.

Victoria Duff
Victoria has worked in education for over 45 years at the district, state, and national levels as a teacher leader, mentor coordinator, grants projects lead, and teacher quality coordinator. During that time, her focus on the importance of professional learning for teaching and learning has provided her with the opportunity to serve as chair of the New Jersey Professional Teachers Standards Board and the Learning Forward Foundation, as well as president of Learning Forward New Jersey. Currently, she serves as Coordinator of Professional Learning, for New Jersey Principals and Supervisors Association and Foundation for Educational Administration where she leads the development and implementation of premier leadership academies and works with educators implementing the Connected Action Roadmap.

Emil Carafa
Emil Carafa has worked in public education for over 41 years at the district level as a Teacher of the Handicapped, elementary school administrator, mentor, coach, president and member of the district, county, and state organizations. A former president of the New Jersey Principals and Supervisors Association (NJPSA), he served as a member Educator Leaders' Cadre for the State of New Jersey, representing NJPSA/FEA administrators at PARCC (Partnership for Assessment of Readiness for College and Careers) on the national level. He was named the 2015 NJPSA Visionary Leader of the Year

Currently, Emil serves as Coordinator of Professional Learning, for the New Jersey Principals and Supervisors Association (NJPSA) and Foundation of Educational Administration (FEA) where he supports educators in the Connected Action Roadmap (CAR) and other educational topics.

# About the Author

A lifelong educator, **Patricia Wright** is the executive director emerita of the New Jersey Principals and Supervisors Association (NJPSA). She is the developer of the Connected Action Roadmap (CAR), a comprehensive and coherent model of school improvement. Pat has held the positions of teacher, reading specialist, assistant principal, principal, and superintendent. She is the recipient of numerous awards including the New Jersey Visionary Principal of the Year Award and the Dr. Ernest Boyer Outstanding Educator Award.

Pat is currently a senior consultant for NJPSA and the Foundation for Educational Administration (FEA). She presents frequently on issues related to CAR, PLCs, school leadership, and school culture and climate.